W9-AHY-379

the

TOAST

always

LANDS

jelly-side

DOWN

the TOAST *always* LANDS *jelly-side* DOWN

and other tales of surburban life

SUZANN LEDBETTER

CROWN PUBLISHERS, INC., NEW YORK

To Paul W. Johns and Debi Williams
for always being there.

Portions of this work have been previously published in various magazines.

Copyright © 1993 by Suzann Ledbetter
Illustrations copyright © 1993 by Monica Sheehan

All rights reserved. No part of this book may be reproduced or transmitted in any form or by any means, electronic or mechanical, including photocopying, recording, or by any information storage and retrieval system, without permission in writing from the publisher.

Published by Crown Publishers, Inc., 201 East 50 Street, New York, New York 10022. Member of the Crown Publishing Group.

Random House, Inc. New York, Toronto, London, Sydney, Auckland

CROWN is a trademark of Crown Publishers, Inc.

Manufactured in the United States of America.

Library of Congress Cataloging-in-Publication Data

Ledbetter, Suzann.
The toast always lands jelly-side down / Suzann Ledbetter.
p. cm.
I. Title.
PN6162.L36 1993
818'.5407—dc20 93-14737
CIP

ISBN 0-517-59552-4

10 9 8 7 6 5 4 3 2 1

First Edition

Contents

THREE: Housework

FOUR: Children

Acknowledgments

My writing career, and this book stemming from it, would not have been possible without my parents, who put me on this planet, taught me that laughter beats tears anytime, and that I can do anything I want if I want it badly enough.

My husband, two sons, and two daughters have not only taken my light-hearted pokes without protest, when I've been on a deadline, they've snarfed more home-delivered pizzas and grilled cheese sandwiches than most people will in a lifetime.

Much of the joy of this profession comes from the wondrous kinship of like-minded scribes. For their encouragement, support, and affection, I'll forever be grateful to Reid Champagne, W.C. Jameson, Paul W. Johns, Vern Modeland, the Tri-County Writers Feedback Group, Jory Sherman, Dale Walker, Debi Williams, and a blessedly long list of friends who've kept me going when it would have been easier to quit.

I'm especially beholden to my mentor, *Family Circle* deputy editor Nancy Clark, Outlet Books editorial director Kate Sheehan Hartson, Crown Publishing Group's Irene Prokop, the most patient, professional editor any writer ever had, and my agent, Alice Orr, for her guidance, good humor, and graciousness.

ONE

IFE

Life is like an

ice-cream cone . . .

you've got to learn to

lick it.

—*Charlie Brown*

Now I Lay Me Down to Sleep, I Hope and Pray My Gown Won't Creep

How can a woman keep the romance alive in her marriage? According to a covey of unwed experts I saw interviewed on a recent afternoon talk show, successfully seductive spouses actually *wear* the lingerie I've always kept wrapped in tissue paper and stuffed in a bottom bureau drawer.

My favorite bedtime ensemble, an oversized football jersey, has never provoked Hubby to compare me to a Heisman trophy candidate, but I couldn't help wondering if The Light of My Life secretly yearned for a wanton wench with a penchant for peignoirs.

Just in case, I decided a change from a casually armchaired quarterback to a soap opera–style siren was in order.

Except, getting all dressed up with nowhere to go was a much more complicated procedure than I had imagined. To begin with, frilly frocks are always tagged with blue-printed labels that sternly command:

> HAND-WASH ONLY. USE A MILD DETERGENT AND RINSE THOROUGHLY WITH LUKEWARM WATER. DO NOT USE CHLORINE BLEACH. DO NOT TWIST, WRING, OR HANG. LAY FLAT TO DRY. TOUCH-UP WITH A COOL IRON MAY BE NECESSARY.

I *will* sink-suds a pricey, cashmere sweater. I *will* iron Spouse's shirt collars and cuffs. After a swim, *I'll* lie flat on a chaise, to dry. But must *all* of the above be done to a garment I merely sleep, perchance to dream, in?

Children presented another glitch in my glamour-girl transformation. Wouldn't I feel a trifle overdressed draped in an Empire-waisted, shimmering shimmy, accessorized with a matching batwing-sleeved, appliquéd satin peignoir and open-toed, stacked-heeled mules while offering maternal assistance to a nine-year-old in the process of pitching his pot roast?

Nor did I expect to hear any appreciative applause if I danced about in a flirty silk chemise, tap pants, and a matching combing coat to serve breakfast featuring crunchy cartoon characters floundering in bowls of pink milk. Undoubtedly, that kind of floor show would be wasted on a decidedly immature audience.

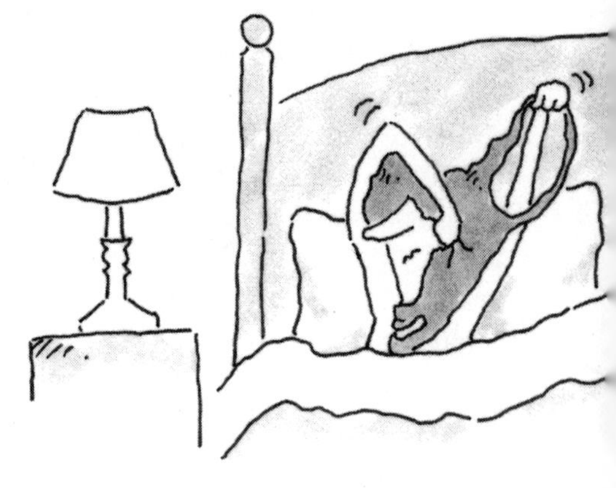

But if romance *was* the name of the game, I'd have to dress the part. While struggling with snaps and straps and back hooks sewn three inches lower than my fingertips' reach induced strains of "It'll Be a Taut Time in the Old Gown Tonight" in my mind, I visualized Himself, dashingly decked in saggy undershorts, humming "Some Enchanted Evening" and awaiting my captivating, curtain-closing premiere. Problem was, by the time the primping was done, My Hero was snoring louder than a bull moose with bad sinuses.

Worse yet, that enticing ensemble later exhibited a frightening resemblance to Count Dracula: Just like a vampire, it rose at midnight and went for my throat. And as the silken skirt crept upward, the skinny shoulder straps fell, and I was rudely awakened by a gown gnarling at my neck and my limbs lassoed like a heifer at the annual Rotary Club Rodeo.

Suffice it to say, loosening this negligeed noose with my hands tied behind my back was an escape attempt worthy of Harry Houdini.

Stubbornly searching for less assault-oriented nightwear, I took the advice of a salestot and purchased a lacy, tank-style "teddy." Only the clerkette failed to warn me that with my torso so tightly entrapped, an innocent sunrise stretch could change this lifelong alto into a lilting soprano.

Rather than waking from a night's hibernation all cute and cuddly like the cub I assumed such garb was named for, I greeted the dawn as grumpy as a grizzly, ready to charge up San Juan Hill. I daresay crotch-snapped jammies are fine for kids unable to stand on their own two feet, but should never have been converted into sort-of adult sizes.

It was apparent Hubby hadn't noticed any of my silver screen starlet debuts or the moonlit manglings I'd suffered, but *was* curious about my sudden insomnia and tendency to nod off during numerous daytime activities.

So, instead of spending the best nights of my life being offensively tackled by homicidal haute couture, I kicked the collection back into the drawer and dressed out again in an extra-large, dual-numeraled football jersey.

Regardless of those theories offered by television talk show "experts," on *my* home field, Coach isn't impressed by my uniform—just my ability to intercept a forward pass.

Mail-order Bride (Only June Cleaver Need Apply)

Grateful as I may be for the efforts of the women's liberation movement, I think there were a couple of planks missing from their well-meaning platform of progress.

First, men have yet to experience the wonders of labor and childbirth. Although there's probably nothing the National Organization of Women can do to change this, the genders can't be equal until the fellas fret about stretch marks, too.

Second, while women have proven themselves able to do a "man's" work, are entitled to a "man's" pay, have been invited to join historically male-membered clubs, and compete in jock-dominated sports, the one luxury most men enjoy and women universally lack . . . is a wife.

By that, I don't mean an able-bodied, salaried female like a maid or nanny. What I want is real, live, carpool-driving, eyes-in-the-back-of-her-head–seeing, bookkeeping, sick-child–nursing, button-sewing, window-washing, meal-fixing, uncomplaining wife. In other words, I want a gal, just like the gal, who married dear old Dad.

If I had a wife, then and only then could I do what the Big Boys do:

- Rely on regular Sunday afternoon tee times because I worked so hard all week.
- Read the entire newspaper without interruption because I worked so hard all day.
- Be guaranteed the best seat in front of the television because I worked so hard to pay for it.

• Plan "can't miss" business conferences whenever parent-supervised Scout overnights are scheduled because my job is so important.

• Forget to pick up the milk, the dry cleaning, or a child on my way home from the office—and be forgiven such omissive sins with hardly more than a sigh because I, after all, have "more pressing" things on my mind.

To even be considered for the position, a wife-for-hire would have to be adept at:

• *Ground Traffic Control:* The ability to navigate four children within three carpools, while ensuring on-time arrival at one daughter's dental appointment, two sons' soccer practices kicking off at opposite ends of town, and a meeting with Other Daughter's teacher who has requested an impromptu conference just to "touch base." This must all be accomplished within a time frame of approximately twenty-seven minutes, and all charges cheerfully delivered to their respective destinations without the designated driver uttering a single obscenity or breaking a traffic law or a blood vessel.

• *Creative Abilities:* Applicants must be able to design and construct prize-winning Halloween costumes from brown paper grocery sacks, paper plates, pipe cleaners, and school glue. Projects may not be begun before midnight, October 30.

Materials for a few tons of play clay, plus poster paint, crayons, paper, glue, and scissors for twelve must always be on hand in the event of a school snow day, so (since she's home anyway) every child in the neighborhood can be entertained, at your house, at no charge.

• *Sewing Skills:* Candidates must be able to do alterations on the *absolutely perfect* prom dress—except it's eleven inches too long, three sizes too big, and simply crying out for a matching fabric sash and puffy sleeves. She must also have the knack for hemming or cuffing boys' pants without making them look "geeky," or creating unsightly lines which will show when they're let down again, about two weeks later.

• *Child Care and Development:* My hired wife wouldn't

mind reading the little ones' favorite book, *Let's Go to the Zoo*, aloud, with appropriate animal noises, every night at bedtime, for three solid months.

She would uphold the highest levels of patience and understanding even if my child:

- Spilled a large tumbler of red-colored fruit drink on the living room's beige carpet where *no* drinks of *any* kind are allowed in the first place.
- Forgot to turn off the hose he drank from last Wednesday, which has left the backyard in perfect condition for hosting the America's Cup Race.
- Put Kitty in the clothes dryer so it won't catch cold after its bath.
- Made homemade lightning bolts by zapping wads of aluminum foil in the microwave.
- Didn't realize she should have asked for permission before volunteering the basement for her senior class's All Night Graduation Party.
- *Money Management Skills:* How to plan and execute a cocktail hour and multicourse gourmet dinner for six clients and their spouses within the amount of time it takes to transport the party home from the airport.

How to buy groceries at a supermarket in a distant town on Monday, so she needn't worry about the check clearing the bank before Wednesday's deposit.

- *Time-Management Talents:* Accurately gauging the amount of time needed to iron an extra-large, heavy-starch-on-the-collar-please man's shirt, stuff four nutritionally balanced lunch bags, weave two sets of waist-length braids, gather and distribute seventeen due-today library books to the appropriate patrons, conjugate a few Spanish verbs, find enough change in purse corners and under the sofa cushions to pay a school lunch charge, diagnose the difference between biology-final flu and flu-flu, and legibly sign two permission slips, one class schedule, and a PTA volunteer cookie request sheet—before the school bus honks.

• *Athletic Ability:* If she can't punt a pigskin, thwack a homer, swish free-throws, do cheerleader splits, skate backward, teach swimming and diving, and leap tall laundry piles in a single bound, she needn't apply.

An applicant must also proclaim an avid fascination with vacuum cleaners, dust rags, toilet bowl brushes, and steam irons. Washing dishes and presoaking a phew hundred sweat socks, scrubbing miles of fingerprinted hallways, and attacking bathroom grout with a toothbrush must induce a beatific bliss bordering on rapture.

Throw in the knowledge of six hundred and twenty-three different ways to prepare ground beef, a firm conviction that houseplants must be watered occasionally, and a sincere attraction to Mr. Rogers as well as all MTV guest performers, and our relationship would be firmly cemented.

Of course, the salary is in the low no-figures, and the contract is devoid of health benefits or retirement clauses. We're also talking twenty-five-hour days, eight-day weeks, with no time off for vacations, holidays, or good behavior. Hospitalization will be considered, however, if arrangements are made well in advance of any medical emergency.

I wonder what would happen if I placed a help wanted ad in my newspaper's classifieds and listed the above requirements?

Within days of publication, I'll bet I couldn't *carry* all the applications from prospective Mail-order Brides I'd find in my mailbox!

Dialing for Duds

Until recently, shopping for new closet deposits meant sweeclacking through a department store's circular chrome racks, trying on several full-priced possibilities, then choosing an ensemble from one of my two favorite designers: Drastically Reduced and Clearance.

I'll admit my purchases may take a while to register, but it's been my experience that salesladies tend to act like temperamental toddlers: If I want them I can't find them. If I don't, they won't leave me alone.

In fact, even on rare occasions when I know exactly what I want and price is no object, the transaction can be an exercise in exasperation.

For example, say I've snared a clerk's full-commissioned attention and am precisely describing my desire for a tailored navy suit of worsted wool. I want the jacket to be fully lined and of classic design, with the skirt hemming a skosh above my kneecaps.

Excitedly, she'll declare, "I've got an outfit in the back that was simply *made* for you." Moments later, she'll burst from the bowels of the stockroom clutching a fussy, floral frock cut from the same cloth as my lawn-chair cushions.

I presume if I were in the market for a big-blossomed blouson, she'd foist a dark blue, double-breasted blazer and skirt on me.

Whether the clerk in question is a Barbie doll–built ingenue or the timeless type uniformed in a basic black dress, a rhinestone brooch glaring above her left breast like a headlamp, matching earbobs, and half-glasses dangling from a neck chain, I don't dare insult the woman in command of the changing rooms. That's the one place where the salesperson's adage "The customer is always right" yields to "The customer is in her underwear and at my mercy."

Her allotment of spacious stalls with knee- to neck-high wooden doors, two brassy wall hooks, and a cat-cornered fake French Provincial chair is reserved for preferred, credit-unlimited patrons—a category in which I've yet to achieve membership.

We cost-conscious consumers are escorted to cramped cubicles with no hooks, no chair, and a flimsy pair of door drapes with a gap at center you could drive a bread truck through.

This absence of finer fixtures and the carpet's veritable minefield of discarded straight pins means I can't safely remove my shoes while trying an ensemble on for size. Suffice it to say, it's difficult to achieve an aura of sophistication when the drapey chiffon cocktail frock I'm modeling is accessorized by bunny-tailed sport socks and road-dirty Reeboks.

Tired of haranguing around with department store protocol, I recently joined the home-shopping network. Comfortably couched with a lap full of mail-order catalogues and a telephone at my side, I can buy everything from pantyhose to formal clothes as easily as my kids phone for a pepperoni pizza. In fact, if mailbox merchandising's popularity continues, it may be possible to get a dialed duds delivery in thirty minutes or less, someday.

Granted, paying a fee for someone to "handle" my ordered outfits before shipping seems a bit strange, and repackaging a pair of too-small snowpants into its mitten-sized return mailer is tricky, but I'm convinced catalogue-shopping is the only way to satisfy my wardrobe requirements.

The selection is almost limitless. The time and stress savings are enormous. And best of all, there's no saleslady to give me a Sweet Tart smile and cackle, "Don't you think that style's a bit *young* for you, dearie?"

What's So Grand About Golf?

According to that respected barometer of public opinion better known as the *Family Feud* answer board, bungee-jumping and hang-gliding were voted the two most "dangerous sports."

While I agree participation in those air-robics smacks of death defiance, I think golf should have made the top ten, too.

After all, using a steel-headed stick to clobber a rock-hard ball and send it hurtling through the air at speeds approaching one hundred and fifty-five miles per hour, in a direction known only to God, is hardly as ho-hum as a tiddlywinks tournament.

As if that's not enough of a challenge, lying between me and a green I can seldom see and only hope to hit are enormous trees, sticker bushes, poison ivy patches, sand pits, scummy ponds, and several very vulnerable human beings.

Although I might learn to play in a less life- and limb-threatening manner, I'm hardly out of the clubhouse before various items of de rigueur attire are causing me problems.

For example: the bunny-tailed sport socks favored by golfers of both genders. I'll grant this footwear is unquestionably comfortable, but its low-slung styling provides no padding whatsoever when my club strays from its intended trajectory and bashes my bare ankle bone.

While reflexively hoisting the injured ankle, hippity-hopping on the other foot, and howling like a lovesick basset hound won't ease my agony, it *is* guaranteed to send my partner's putt winging into another area code.

And no one bothered to warn me not to cross my legs when my feet were decked in spike-soled golf shoes. Too late I learned that the same gleaming fangs I counted on to anchor me to terra firmly can plow furrows in my shins deep enough to sow soybeans.

Even golf-oriented shorts and slacks, which come factory-equipped with gigantic fore pockets (as opposed to aft) so tees, divot fixers, ball markers, and scoring pencils can be kept handy at all times, can seriously wound the unwary. By about the twelfth hole, those britches are bulging with the accumulated pointy-ended accoutrements, and bending too hastily may result in the puncturing of several internal organs. No wonder many golf enthusiasts hire caddies to do the groundwork for them.

OK, so there are millions who'll insist that dethatching a landmass the size of Ben Cartwright's Ponderosa is the closest thing to heaven on earth. Thousands will scoff at the notion of apparel endangerment, and snottily dismiss me as a chronically clumsy grump who doesn't deserve the delights of frequent foreplay.

But I'll bet not a one can satisfactorily explain,
Why, if this game is really so tame,
That "golf," I mean its very name,
Is nothing but "flog" spelled backward.

Hi Ho, Silver...

To me, gray hairs are like paychecks. Just because I'm getting them regularly doesn't mean I want to show them to everyone.

When I was younger and my hair was considerably darker, I vowed to never tint my tresses. I thought gray hair and wrinkles were natural, and my attitude was natural for one who had neither.

As with many mothers, the silver sprouted at about the same time my children became teenagers. The first whitish wisps were easy to disguise, but an eventual bumper crop soon caught the light *and* my attention.

My husband's hair was graying faster than my own, but his was a distinguished shade of sterling silver. My pewterish patches were about as attractive as lint on a dark sweater.

Determined to find the fountain of youth at my drugstore, I scanned the inventory of two hundred and forty-one types of hair-coloring products.

The first thing I noticed were the words "New!" "Easy," "Peroxide & Ammonia Free!" and "Body-Building Formula," boldly printed on the front of every package. I was certainly thankful that the old, difficult, peroxide & ammonia–chocked, wimpy stuff foisted on prior generations was no longer available.

I was also dazed by the range of shades. Except "Marvelously Mink" seemed a bit chichi for a Midwestern mother of four. "Flaming Vixen" might set off our smoke alarms. "Shimmering Champagne" was too light, "Majestic Mahogany" too much like a furniture finish, and "Midnight Raven" was for the birds. Nowhere was the shade I sought: Basic Brown.

Just as I resigned myself to dull-headed dowagership, I spotted a coloring kit designed to only highlight hair. The mixture was supposed to be brushed on and promised to change individual strands from gray to glimmering. Who could ask for more?

Draped in one of Hubby's ugliest favorite shirts, I had just enough time to dabble on the dye before the school bus dropped off the children.

The first clues that this process might not be as easy as advertised was an enormous sheet of sternly worded "Cautions" attached to a pair of plastic gloves similar to those used by a crew cleaning up a toxic waste dump.

Then, when mixing my magic paint potion, its aroma immediately brought back memories of my childhood. It smelled exactly like the frog I dissected in eighth-grade biology class.

Not one to let little things like terror and noxious fumes stand in the way of progress, I proceeded to paint my umber over every smoky strand. And I splattered a smidge here and there for a more overall effect. Glimmering wasn't enough—I wanted to *dazzle.*

After waiting the prescribed period (more or less), I rinsed, slathered on the creamy conditioner, rinsed again until drowning was a distinct possibility, and fluffed my hair with a blow-dryer.

Expecting a lion-maned lassie to be reflected in my mirror, it came as quite a shock to see a cat of a different color. Many different colors. Granted, the gray was gone, but changing into a tricolored tabby was not the effect I'd hoped to create.

Because my children's reaction ranged from uncontrollable laughter to remarks such as "Daddy's gonna CROAK when he sees you!" I was left with two choices: either spend the next two months with my head swathed in a babushka, or buy the shampoo-in rinse I should have used in the first place.

Choosing Plan 2, I dashed back home with the tint closest

to my original hair color and went through all the smelly motions again.

But in my haste to undo the damage, I neglected to read a paragraph that warned: "Previously color-treated or highlighted hair may absorb more color. Results may be darker than expected."

And darker was indeed what my hair changed, but from what I've been told, by double-dosing my hair in one day, I'm lucky I still have some. At least my dye job has resolved who Hubby and I will be for our neighborhood's annual Halloween party.

Since I already look like Tonto, Hubby will just have to go as the Lone Ranger.

Noble Intentions

In these health-oriented times, cutting calories, cholesterol, and other toothsome food features from my diet is a noble intention. Unfortunately, like too many of my other noble intentions, this one's getting skewed by economic reality.

I found that not only are many supermarketed morsels labeled "lite," "diet," "lean," or "low calorie/salt/sugar/cholesterol/fat" about as tasty as the containers they come in, they're priced considerably higher than their heavy/fattening/robust/high-calorie/salt/sugar/cholesterol-choked counterparts.

Assumably, the establishment of this "less is more" concept started years ago when consumers didn't question why unleaded gasoline was more expensive than leaded regular, even though lead is a petroleum *additive.* As a result, the notion that the more things a product claims it *doesn't* have, the more it costs, gained general acceptance.

Best I can figure, every "No ———" deletion proclaimed on a package raises its retail price by approximately 20 percent. That's why producers of naturally fat-free foods are no longer hiding their "lites" under bushels—they're simply charging more for them.

Similarly, fresh fruit and vegetable marketeers are squeezing cash out of health-conscious customers. Whenever I see Day-Glo-ing signs fluttering above bins of "organically grown" merchandise, I know their multidigited, per-pound prices are going to set my heart all aflutter, as well.

While health-fanatic friends wax poetically on the virtues of nonchemically produced produce, they'll invariably season those slices of organically grown tomatoes with a sprinkling of salt substitute. Does this mean granulated dashes of potassium chloride, potassium bitartrate, adipic acid, mineral oil, and fumaric acid don't count as chemicals, if added post–pick 'em?

Ditto slathering OrGrown corncobs with nonbutter substances concocted of maltodextrin, natural butter flavor(?), salt, spray dried butter, guar gum, and baking soda. Or sweetening strawberried bowls of regularity flakes with compounds containing lactose, aspartame, maltodextrin, leucine, cellulose, and cellulose derivatives.

Maybe I'm missing the point, but to me, that makes as much sense as washing down a double cheeseburger, jumbo fries, and a deep-fried pie with a diet soda.

In addressing the meat of this issue, a spokesperson for the American Dietetic Association recommends only beef and pork cuts carrying "round" or "loin" in the name (sir*loin*, tender*loin*, eye of *round*, *round* steak) and ground *round* or sir*loin* for hamburgers. Except the ADA didn't explain how my family's bologna-ranged budget should finance such primo provisions. As a mother of four, including a six-foot-five, 240-pound, voraciously carnivorous son, if "round steak" is on the menu, it comes with mustard, relish, catsup, and an elongated bun.

And the skinless chicken and fish suggested as alternatives? To say they're expensive is an understatement. For that kind of money, the chicken had better have been a golden-egg layer, and the fish, directly descended from the miraculous pair that fed the biblical multitudes.

Nevertheless, I do heartily agree with the government's concept of a "healthier food lifestyle" for all. Survival of the fittest is not only stylish again; considering the alternative, longevity wins every time. In fact, I'll be as pleased as hundred-percent fruit punch to jump on that do-right diet bandwagon—just as soon as the Loot Fairy slips enough legally tender lettuce under my pillow to pay for the provisions.

Someday You're Gonna Get *It*

After days of suffering mucous membrane malfunction, a throat seared like an apprentice fire-eater's, crimson-rimmed eyes, and an eardrum-rattling cough, I abandoned all attempts at home health care and called the doctor.

I considered pleading for a physician's intervention at the onset of this illness, but being a proud, do-it-myself and save-a-few-bucks American, I tried the more traditional method first: swallowing potentially lethal combinations of alphabetized vitamins followed by supermarketed potions promising no less than twelve hours of relief, rest, and unobstructed respiration.

Unfortunately, other than an irresistible urge to nod off suddenly or to ease excessive hypertension by bench-pressing a pickup, these home-dosed nostrums did little to dispel my discomfort. It was time to bring in a professional.

After kindly Dr. Wellbe tested my gag reflex by probing numerous orifices with enormous mutant Q-Tips, beat on my back with his bent-knuckled old fists, and "hmmmed" and "ah hahed" around awhile, he diagnosed my distress as the highly contagious *It.*

Wellbe added that I was but one of many *It*-carrying casualties he had recently examined, and that his wife was just recovering from *It.* As a matter of fact, he wasn't feeling so frisky himself all of a sudden.

After penning a prescription guaranteed to cost approximately forty-seven dollars but not guaranteed to affect a cure, he instructed me to go home to bed, drink plenty of liquids, and not breathe upon anyone of whom I was fond.

As I drug myself through the pneumatic doors of the drugstore (an emporium not named for a pharmaceutically oriented inventory, but for the sluggishness of its customers), I was hailed heartily by the woman who unquestionably inspired the "Good fences make good neighbors" axiom.

"Gosh, what's the matter with you?" she asked, adding, "You look *awful*!"

In reply to her keen observational powers I wheezed, "My doctor says I've got *It*, and *It* is extremely contagious. Perhaps you should back off, oh, a hundred yards or so, before my germs jump you and start mutilating several vital internal organs."

"Oh, don't worry," she assured, "I've already had *It* and believe you me, if you're well enough to run around town, you aren't *nearly* as sick as *I* was!"

With her voice reaching decibel levels more common to those calling hogs to a trough, she itemized her own *It* list, including (but not limited to) a Guinness record-breaking fever, leg paralysis, dermatitis, bronchitis, skull-busting headaches, and abdominal cramping much like those Mrs. Jumbo experienced the day she birthed Dumbo.

"Believe me, you're lucky you only have a *touch* of *It*," she trumpeted.

After expressing my appreciation for her unsolicited insights and remarking that the next time I felt like *It*, I would certainly think of her, I pocketed my pills and stumbled homeward to compose my Last Will and Testament.

Contrary to popular belief, misery does not always love company—especially sort-of sympathetic family members who shook me regularly to inquire, "Are you asleep?" "Aren't you feeling better *yet*?" "Do we have to cook our own dinner *again*?" and "Where's my paisley tie/library books/Intergalactic Star Warrior Decoder Ring/Vise-grips/little brother?"

However, during one semi-lucid interlude when a prior dosage of medication had waned and the next not quite taken effect, I made an astounding medical discovery: If an anatomical distress carries multisyllabic terminology, a cure can be immediately administered and the recovery period is incredibly short.

I've known heart bypass recipients (in Medispeak: a reverse saphenous vein aortocoronary bypass graft) who were cruising hospital corridors the day after such death-defying surgery.

But if my system is plagued by the singularly syllabled *It*, regardless of all the scientific advances of this century, *nothing* quells the queasiness quickly.

Seems to me that until the medical community assigns *It* a totally unpronounceable name, I'll have to use the same wellness barometer that's *always* gotten me off my hands and knees and back on my feet again: the instinct to survive, and the number of paid "sick days" allowed per annum.

Breastbone Billboards

So you want to inspire, inform, or lend a chuckle to the general public? Don't bother renting a billboard or writing letters to congresspersons and newspaper editors. You can more easily entertain humankind by exhibiting meaningful messages or promotional propaganda on a T-shirt.

It's amazing how much can be learned about total strangers just by reading the writing on their chests. Loyal fans advertise their regard for a variety of professional or collegiate athletic organizations by flaunting the colorful logos of their favorites. Beachside pleasure palaces, ski resorts, national parks, amusement centers, gambling casinos, and spas offer overpriced gift-shop shirts emblazoned with screenprinted graphics advertising their particular piece of tourist heaven.

Any observer of such souvenired attire may not know who you are, but will know where you spent your summer vacation and major quantities of disposable income.

Lifeless, stick-in-the-mud homebodies who'll forever pet-sit, pick up the travelers' mail and newspapers, and watch over vacant houses undoubtedly have drawers full of "My Friends Tanned in Tampa (Surfed at Big Sur/Schussed at Snowmass, etc.) and All I Got Is This Lousy T-Shirt(s)" received in appreciation of their guardianship.

Curiously, parents who wouldn't wipe insect remains from a windshield with such garish garments *will* buy the child-sized versions. This is because even the tackiest T-shirt is a more practical remembrance of Family Fun in the Sun than multijointed plastic reptiles or genuine Native American squaw dolls manufactured in minor Asian countries.

And what of shirts proclaiming wearers as breed-specific dog lovers, grandmas, grandpas, beer swillers, Elvis forever faithfuls, or cartoon character/rock singer/motorcycle fans? Unscientific study has shown this segment of the population to drive gun-racked, duck-decaled pickup trucks equipped with ill-fitting camper shells, to contribute to Brother Lee Love's evangelistic organization, and to landscape their lawns with discarded plumbing fixtures planted with petunias.

Then there are those who believe they have something to say, a fifty-fifty cotton-and-polyester blended right to say it, and a collection of "message" shirts to prove it. Remarkably, our culture has rapidly advanced from wearing our hearts on our sleeves to pasting our fuzzy-lettered beliefs on our bosoms.

Examples of such brilliance, marketed in a variety of sizes, colors, and reduced-for-clearance prices include:

• "If You Love Something, Set It Free. If It Comes Back, Kill It" (chosen primarily by parents of delinquent adolescents).

• "PMS Is Sexist" (true, but so are prostate problems).

• "Objects Beneath May Be Larger Than They Appear" (this public service announcement is limited to shirts; it is unlikely to be embroidered upon the back pocket of blue jeans).

• "Nobody's Prefect" (One of my personal favorites).

• "A Camel Is a Horse Designed by Committee" (definitely the former chairperson of a nonprofit organization).

• "Two Wrongs Don't Make a Right, But Three Lefts Do" (guaranteed to stump some readers for a second or two; others, pretty much forever).

• "Buy American" (invariably shimmering in patriotic red, white, and blue on garments imported from Taiwan).

• "If You're Rich, I'm Single" (that one's enough to make celibacy seem doable, isn't it?).

• "It Takes Studs to Build Houses" (and some of us are short a few two-by-fours in the old woodpile, too).

• "Money Talks . . . Mine Says 'Goodbye' " (an upper-bracketed income earner with no dependents and a leaky tax shelter).

• "Don't Yell at Me. I Didn't Vote for Him" (only in America will people pay good money for a shirt proclaiming their continued support of the last election's loser).

• "Baby on Board" (either a maternity T or worn by the parent of a toddler who's a surfing fanatic).

• "Don't Tell Me What Kind of Day to Have" (definitely slows the frequency of "Have a nice day"s).

While I refuse to pay for the privilege of having my attire provide free advertising for products or services, I'll admit a pithy remark often blurbs boldly from my frontage.

Hey, why not put your money where *your* mouth was and make some T-shirty fashion statements, too? If for no other reason, it's really a hoot seeing folks get all flush-faced and embarrassed when you catch them staring at your chest.

Pair-or-Less Situation

Noah had the right idea when he loaded his ark with pairs of all the creatures on earth. Two by two, with future repopulation in mind, passengers loped, crawled, and flew aboard to weather the storm.

As a descendant of Noah, I therefore assume a pair of something to mean two of them. A pair of bunnies in the backyard means two animals grazing in the garden. A pair of wet socks left on the bed means two soggy spots, plus one son in a ton of trouble.

If a pair should equal two, then why do packages enumerating undergarments as "three *pairs*" yield only three garments instead of six? Pantyhose are enveloped as pairs too, but surrender only one wad of tinted nylon.

Further investigation reveals more inconsistencies than answers.

If a man shops for new socks, he purchases a pair of two socks, not individual items of footwear. We wear pairs (two) of shoes, and pairs (two) of earrings, yet a pair of eyeglasses fit only one nose.

While mulling this revelation, I tried to figure out why clothing is thought of as paired whether the number of individual items would equal one or two. Could it be that underwear and slacks are "pairs" because of the number of appendages inserted through openings?

This seemed a logical explanation until the same theory was applied to a shirt. If one counts armholes, shirts should be bought in singularly termed pairs, too.

A different Noah, the *Webster's Dictionary* daddy, defined a pair as "two corresponding things designed for use together," and the entry cites trousers to illustrate its meaning.

I'd ask wise Webster why his description is only accurate when referring to socks, underwear, slacks, and pantyhose, yet the same theory is not applicable to sweaters, shirts, and overcoats—but he cashed in his quill about a hundred and fifty years ago.

I find this tangle of terminology curious, but imagine what confusion it could cause an innocent immigrant. If Peter Piper, a new resident of our land, went into a department store to purchase some American clothing, I can only imagine the resulting conversation:

CLERK: "How may I help you, sir?"

PETER: "I want to buy jean, shirt, and pair of socks."

CLERK: "Fine, let's start with the jeans. How many pairs do you need?"

PETER: "I do not want a pair, I just want one."

CLERK: "Er, one *what*, sir?"

PETER: "One jean."

CLERK: "You mean, one *pair* of jeans."

PETER: "No! I learned in English class that one pair equals two things. I cannot afford more than one jean today."

CLERK: "Ah, now I understand. You see, sir, in this country, we call them a *pair* of jeans because of the two legs. A *pair* of jeans is just one garment. Do you understand?"

PETER: "Yes, thank you. A pair of jeans is just one. Okay, then I also want two pairs of socks."

CLERK: "Two pairs of socks coming up."

PETER: "Wait! There are *four* socks in your hand. I have only two feet, so I only want two pairs."

CLERK: "But sir, this *is* two pairs. A pair of socks is one sock for each foot."

PETER: "I thought you said a pair was only one?"

CLERK: "Well, that's true for jeans because you cannot buy trousers of any kind with just one leg in them, but socks are just as you said earlier—a pair of socks *two* socks."

PETER: "This is all very strange. I ask for socks as one pair of two socks. I ask for jean as one pair too, because they have two legs. Let me think just a minute, I want to get it correct this time. . . . For my final purchase I want a *pair* of shirts. One shirt, two arms; a pair, right?"

Noah or Noah Webster? Which pundit's principle should Peter Piper pick?

Shoulding, Musterbation, and Hardening of the Oughteries

I don't smoke anymore, never have been much of a drinker, but I still have three mighty bad habits I can't seem to shake. When I'm not Shoulding on myself, I'm either Musterbating or suffering from Clogged Oughteries.

None has ever sped a domestic or professional assignment to completion, but all chronic conditions are quite handy during interludes of burgeoning self-pity.

"Shoulding on myself" comes in handy when I'm mulling over supposed parenting or household deficiencies: "I *should* cook dinner tonight instead of phoning for pizza." "I *should* have read the children another bedtime story." "I *should* be reviewing tomorrow's meeting agenda, not watching television." "I *should* spend Saturday cleaning the house instead of attending that seminar."

It matters little whether a delivered dinner is the family's fare of choice, that by virtue of my children's procrastination storytime is *always* singular, that even the groaniest sitcom is more entertaining than office homework, or that any opportunity for expanding my professional skills supersedes vacuuming and dusting. Still, I somehow feel it's my duty as an achievement-oriented American to give myself a verbal lashing with a litany of guilt-edged words.

If not Shoulding, I "Musterbate": "I *must* get that promotion or I'll never have another chance." "I *must* attend all twenty-seven dress rehearsals of my daughter's preschool play lest she think I am disinterested in her extracurricular activities."

"I *must* go to the cleaners, the bank, the post office, and find a party dress during my lunch hour even if I'm starved and will be chomping diet-dooming candy bars by 2:00 P.M."

Musterbation is as addictive as heroin and just about as healthy. Worrying endlessly about trivialities seldom gets my tasks in gear, and most Musterbations are simply not that important. When I'm thinking rationally, I realize this frustrating mental overdrive is like being the fourth person to climb Mount Everest. The reason no one remembers who accomplished that feat fourth is because it didn't really matter much except to the climber.

Inviting friends for sit-down suppers, writing my mother, coaching a son's soccer team or volunteering for another's homeroom duties, reading *War and Peace*, saving more, spending less, losing ten pounds, and organizing our walk-in closet so we can actually walk in it is but a random sampling of the six hundred and forty-one "Oughteries" clogging my peace of mind.

I habitually begin the year by listing dozens more, commonly known as New Year's Resolutions. Those notes are then posted prominently so I can be reminded of my continuing inadequacies on a daily basis.

Truth to tell, if I kicked the butt of the person most responsible for producing the high-stress episodes I often experience, I wouldn't be able to sit down for weeks.

I don't know if I'll ever be free of Shoulding on myself, Musterbation, or Oughtery Clogging, but I'm going to try my darnedest to make them more a memory than a millstone.

And I'm going to tackle this Personal Improvement Plan really soon, but I *should* get the ironing caught up, I *must* finish that proposal before the sales meeting next week, and I *ought* to take the kids on that canoe trip I promised . . . first.

Sign Language

During a recent minivacation, since it was neither dark of night nor raining torrentially, and therefore not my turn to drive, I found myself studying "sign language."

The first thing I noticed was a smattering of "Hill" signs heralding what I'd always considered major, and highly visible, topographical irregularities. That I shared Life's Highways with others who must be *told* of up- and down-going terrain was a frightening concept.

After all, if a fellow traveler didn't notice a Hill hunkering on the horizon, just what assurance did I have that he or she would see the *sign*?

For no particularly good reason, highway departments are replacing many of the old-fashioned worded warnings with geometric symbols much like those found in *Teach Your Toddler Math* manuals.

That's why pictographs of fishtailing auto posteriors are becoming more common than "Slippery When Wet" signs. Replacing "Ped Xing," an admittedly confusing abbreviation, is a silhouetted personage (albeit one with no neck, feet, or hands) to signify a "Pedestrian Crossing."

Due to the number of markers illustrated by an antlered animal and captioned "Deer Crossing" in bold black lettering, I presume Bambi Brigades were commissioned to determine exactly where deer ford streams of oncoming traffic, and such signs were posted accordingly.

Or, maybe the deer just mosey along until they spot a species-specific sign indicating the proper crosswalk. If so, then no *wonder* chickens have always had such a tough time crossing the road—they've lacked the proper signage.

Despite these classic examples, translating sign language into symbolism is hardly universal, because some highway hazards have proven difficult to depict. While darned if I know how they'll ever draw a "Dead End," the following suggestions came to mind and might be doable:

Since "Bump" and "Dip" signs are invariably placed approximately nine inches before the corresponding heave or hollow, a picture of shattered shock absorbers could be an appropriate substitute. Then again, since not everyone recognizes pulverized auto parts when they see them, due to the heights and depths one's soul does reach when traversing these "surface irregularities," I propose a caricature of a driver with an expression of abject terror and eyes the size of turkey platters. Sets of spurs crossed like rapiers in the corners would leave no doubt that a "Dip" was approaching.

"Impassable During High Water" warnings are often posted along county roads in my part of the country. Unfortunately, the hand-painted gauges usually staked beside them seldom note which hash mark is considered "High," i.e., "Impassable."

To give motorists a better idea whether to proceed full steam ahead or drop anchor, I think flippers should be added at about axle level, goggles at around door-handle depths, and a bubble-pluming snorkel indicative of over-the-roof-so-kiss-it-goodbye rampages.

Further, many bridge builders must follow sets of one-size-fits-all blueprints, since so many *two*-laned country roads feature "One-lane Bridge Ahead"s. Although playing Get-Across-Before-That-Oncoming-Hay-Truck adds thrills and chills to any scenic shortcut, perhaps a skull and crossbones would better forewarn that a stretch of anorexic asphalt lurks up yonder.

A vehicle smashed to smithereens beneath a megatonned boulder ought to get the "Falling Rock" message across. Only, suppose I *did* notice a chunk of limestone wanking down from the heavens? A second sign advising what defensive driving technique to employ to avoid being crushed to dust would be incredibly helpful. After all, being caught between a rock and a hard place is no time to ponder precautionary procedures.

Lastly, although this peeve has nothing to do with symbolic substitution, it does point out another teensy oversight in need of correction—specifically, those gargantuan green signboards promising "FOR EMERGENCY HELP CALL 1-800-000-000."

While I appreciate the thoughtfulness and security the message conveys, and I thank the highway department for providing a toll-free call to someone who cares, wouldn't it be a nice touch if an actual, functional phone was installed within a mile or ten of the @#$%&*% sign?

I've Got a Secret

Sorry, Carolina, but *nothing* could be finer than to be a home-based writer . . . in the morning, or anytime. Except I did make a small mistake in home-office ownership: I announced it to the neighbors.

No sooner were these daytime absentee homeowners apprised of my writer-in-residence status than my address became better known to UPS employees, school bus drivers, merchandise deliverers, and latchkey kids (who forgot theirs) than 1600 Pennsylvania Avenue.

Within weeks, my home was the habitat where surrounding humanity dropped parcels and progeny for pickup later. And according to the school nurse, twenty-seven parents named me as their "in case of emergency" contactperson.

Suffice it to say, "The more one gives, the more one will receive" can be interpreted in more ways than one.

Next, without my knowledge or consent, I was elected Subdivisional Keeper of the Keys, defined as: she who is *always* available to unlock nine-to-fivers' doors for appliance repairs, carpet shampooings, and furniture deliveries.

Neighborly chatterers who once greeted me with "Hi! How are you?" were more often prefacing conversations with "Since you're home all day anyway, would you mind . . . ?"

Grudgingly, I accepted these perpetual interruptions as the price one paid for domesticated employment, but then another type of pestilence started skewing my work schedule.

Like locusts in July, the borrowers came a-swarming and carried away typing paper, manila envelopes, postcards, and

postage stamps. Obviously, the buggers believed I grew that stuff like okra and needn't traipse all over town replenishing *my* office-supply pantry.

Others heard that my reference books were chock-full of facts needed for school-agers' due-tomorrow history reports. Unlike public libraries established for that purpose, I kept flexible hours and the date for returning purloined publications was perceived as any month featuring a blue moon.

Even my computer turned traitorous. I was the only user it was supposed to befriend, but it got turned on every time a mere acquaintance needed to mail-merge an organizational membership list or spread-sheet quarterly income taxes.

By now, my output was at best Reaganomic (trickling down steadily), yet my Good Neighbor policy escalated until someone had the audacity to borrow my computer's portently compatible *keyboard.*

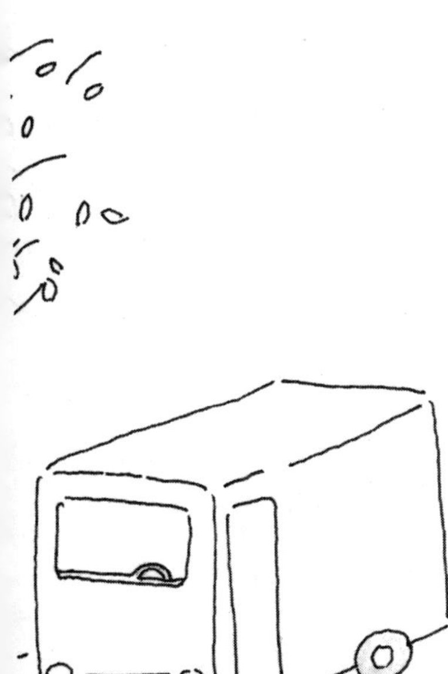

"Stupid me," that someone chortled (and I concurred), "I spilled coffee on mine and shorted it out. But I've got some *really* important work to do, so you wouldn't mind if I borrowed *yours*, would you?"

I will leave the essence of my reply to the reader's imagination. However, that supercilious mooch actually did me a favor: His total inconsideration of my professional priorities finally stiffened my flimsy backbone.

With consistent nay-saying and chronic doorbell deafness, I was eventually able to cease answering every neighbor's beck and call.

To those experiencing similar difficulties, I offer this advice: Stroll to the mailbox in mules and boa-trimmed lingerie. Keep all drapes drawn and doors locked. Smile coquettishly when asked what you do all day.

The neighbors might call you *wanton*, but that's better than constantly calling you *wanting*.

What's the Password?

I can't cure my memory typewriter's chronic amnesia; I don't understand how a VCR tapes programs when the television is *off*; and automated teller machines invariably munch my identification card but rarely regurgitate cash.

So, as a lifelong member of the Technologically Illiterate segment of our society, predictions of tomorrow's *Star Trek*-ish *Smart Cars* were not met with my boundless enthusiasm.

According to four-wheeling forecasters, robotic eyes designed to scan the horizon and warn of highway hazards will be available soon. While this is touted as an accident-prevention device, I'm convinced the *Titanic*'s captain would have shared my skepticism. After all, knowing *what* one is about to whomp isn't nearly as important as knowing *how* to get one's aft out of the way.

On-board computers guiding drivers to unfamiliar destinations are also in the foreseeable future. For those who believe this a cure for the Unmarked Exit Ramp Blues, please note that nationwide, over nineteen thousand roads were either built, barricaded, rerouted, or renumbered last year *alone*.

Speaking as one who hasn't a clue how to program a microwave's meat probe and doesn't care to learn, keypunching countless road corrections would be just what I need: another full-time job.

Satellite-signaled navigators will be available after these on-board computers, but since similar telephone technology is already on-line, I ponder its proficiency, as well. For example, what if hundreds of straying travelers tuned into the satellite simultaneously? Due to an immediate "system overload," a Buick in Boston could accidently intercept the beam intended for a New Yorker's Nissan. Suffice it to say, precise directions to the Empire State Building would send those Beantown tourists on a major wild-goose chase.

Those keyless, voice-activated door locks give me pause for thought, too. Envisioning myself carrying on a passwordy conversation with a keyhole is bad enough, but what happens when the flu alters my natural alto to a raspy bass?

I rue the day I find myself stuck in a parking lot, probably in the drizzling rain, pleading like a dripping puppy with a tone deaf, coldhearted voice monitor that just says "No."

Yet, there are some things techno-wizardry cannot change. For safety's sake, a driver's viewing enjoyment will forever be focused on billboards, pasture-ized cattle, and roadside rock formations. It's the backseaters who'll someday be entertained by miniature televisions, personal computers, and video games. But before such gimcracks become standard equipment, I dare any research and development engineer to survive a two-week vacation with two children—one who's continually zingo-bleeping intergalactic invaders and another who's mesmerized by, and singing along with, a hundred and twelve consecutive hours of MTV—trapped in the backseat together. No doubt a literal understanding of the term "driven insane" would result.

Come on, Detroit—before cars with IQ's higher than their monthly payments start rolling off assembly lines, how about giving serious thought to the features most folks prefer in their cars: running, and paid for.

Oh, Give Me a Home Perm

Oh, give me a home perm,
Where the curls and waves roam firm,
And the style and the body will stay,
Where seldom is heard,
A blasphemous word,
As my scalp becomes toxic sauté.

After spending several long, hair-raising afternoons in beauticians' bibs, my neck bruised by sink edges and paying enormous sums for the privilege, I decided to try curling my own hair, at home.

The array of supermarketed curling kits was daunting. Some promised to provide bouncingly beautiful body, others a kinder, gentler wave. My final decision was based on the method I've always used to choose cosmetics and undergarments: I bought the brand with the prettiest model on the front, even though this strategy has yet to affect my complexion or my cleavage.

Thinking myself all ready to roll, I was surprised to discover the advertised "Super Simple" instructional diagram was only slightly smaller than a king-size *quilt*, and listed, in finely printed purple ink, "Ninety-nine Steps to a Perfect Perm."

I've always believed that any situation involving ninety-nine steps should be avoided, but my quest for curls had gone too far to heed the wisdom of experience.

I'll admit I skipped several of the more basic hair-*do*'s, but two of the boldly highlighted DON'TS did catch my attention.

First, I was told the Abominable Snowman–sized gloves were *not* optional equipment. It seems that foul-smelling formulas designed to cure my hair's straightforward tendencies might also cause skin rashes, strip furniture, and tarnish jewelry if dribbled about carelessly. It was not until I had spread an acre or so of industrial-grade tarpaulins over every conceivably vulnerable surface that I questioned what the perming potion might do to my *head.*

I began to regard the chemical's spout-topped bottle as a miniature Molotov cocktail after noting a gigantically lettered "DO NOT USE NEAR FIRE OR FLAME." Smokers, apparently, are doomed to straight hair.

I was determined to obey the manufacturer's every command to the letter, but the process of rolling my hair on the rods was almost beyond me: My tresses stubbornly refused to be paper-trained. Alas, the instructions failed to mention that

extraordinary patience, manual dexterity befitting a microsurgeon, and a thick, lockable door to muffle muttered profanities were also required before my hair could be successfully harnessed.

Finally, with each rod wound (more or less), I stuck my head in the sink and doused each wad with the magic curling lotion. This step sounded simple, but I managed to fill both ear canals, shoot a spine-chilling stream down my back, and feel toxic tidal waves rolling toward my eyes before I successfully squirted any of the target areas.

With my head bagged in plastic like a leaking rump roast, and reeling from self-induced fumigation, I telephoned the perm product's toll-free "HELP!" number to get either professional aid or calming reassurance. To my dismay, the call was answered by a "No longer in service" recording.

The 911 dispatcher I awakened next was sympathetic, but did not believe my predicament was a true medical emergency requiring helicoptered paramedics.

By then it was time to unwind anyway. Naturally, the curlers, which had failed to get a firm grip earlier, clung tenaciously to each tendril. I yanked and tugged and before long, a cotillion of frizzy fur balls was waltzing across the bathroom counter.

After slathering on about a quart of post-trauma conditioner and rinsing with a few hundred gallons of lukewarm water, the towel-dried New Me turned out *not* to be a twin of the fourteen-year-old nymphet smiling from the product's package. *I* looked like a kennel-clipped French poodle.

OK, I *know* the word "permanent" is hardly accurate when defining the effects of a chemical hair curl. I *know* the waving process is, at best, only temporary.

But if my upwardly mobile locks don't "relax" soon, I'll be forced to paste perky plaid bows over my ears and change my name to Fifi.

Rainin' Rats and Hogs

In my estimation, rudeness is inflating faster than the South American economy, and I'm not referring to the absence of "pleases," "thank-yous," or "excuse-mes." An ever-increasing percentage of our population is behaving as if basic graciousness went out with bobby sox and Bobby Vinton.

The most pronounced and potentially dangerous perpetrators of such ill-mannerism are a two-party automotive minority: Rats and Hogs. Naturally, my worst days seem to spawn these beasts of the boulevard to a point where I'd swear it's *rainin'* Rats and Hogs. Any driver should recognize the species.

A Hog hunkering on your back bumper is as aggravating as a mosquito bite between the shoulder blades. Not only will a Hog threaten you with the equivalent of a vehicular one-night stand at every intersection, it'll turn arrogantly *left* well after the signal glows red, or squeeze between curbs and cars thereby plowing a customized, right-turn lane.

A Hog's horn-honking reflex activates within a millisecond of a light's change to green, and this breed of swine believes mental telepathy is a workable substitute for directional signals.

Because I know I'm insured, but don't know whether the Road Hog is, these close encounters test my defensive driving skills to the limit, and make me want to kick myself for dropping those Tae Kwon Do classes last winter.

The Rats, on the other hand, may gleefully ricochet through traffic, or wait until you're a scootch shy of the intersection before pulling out in front of your car, but primarily, they frequent major metropolitan parking areas.

Rats are the pests who try to limp convincingly after pirating a "Handicapped Only" space. If all those special sections are taken by those for whom they were intended, the Rat will center its adored sports car in *two* parking spaces, to keep it a safe distance from neighboring cars' doors and their dimpling dings.

But the most homicide-inspiring trick a Rat commits carries this modus operandi: Patiently, I'm cruising aisle after aisle of parked autos, praying for a vacancy. Suddenly, I spot a pair of back-up lights flashing just ahead. With a grateful sigh, I'll brake some distance from the dearly departing to allow her plenty of room to navigate.

Except just as she's straightening her wheels to exit, a Rat appears out of nowhere and zizzes dead-bang into MY parking space. Then the execrable little Roadent has the *cojones* to wave jauntily as he makes his way to the mall. All I gain is an instantaneous comprehension of what constitutes "temporary insanity."

When my temper cools, I remember that *most* folks are of the kind and courteous variety, but the Hogs and Rats of the road are enough to make me pine for a James Bond–like sedan. Equipped with an oil-slick dispenser and a tire slasher, I could retaliate without batting an eyelash. And, although it shames me to admit it, I *could* take on a "two can play THAT game, heh-heh-heh" attitude and obliterate a few tires, or start wanking through traffic as obnoxiously as they do.

Without a doubt, Rats and Hogs make it easy to understand why aspirin's pain-relieving qualities were recognized within a few years of the automobile's invention.

Mirror, Mirror on the Wall . . .

In the movies and on television, women always awaken radiantly rested—as lovely as a dew-kissed flower. The only floral tribute that comes to mind when I face *my* morning mirror is the corsage I saved from my Senior Prom: both Mom and mum are wilted, wrinkled, and obviously past their prime.

Applying approximately a hundred and twenty-seven dollars' worth of cosmetics to achieve that "natural look" and winding spaghetti-limp hair around hot rods does help renovate the wreckage. Yet even if the bathroom mirror reflects its approval of the head-and-shoulders view, a full-length fault-detector in yonder closet lurks.

Clamping that head-to-toe foe to the inside of my closet door was supposed to allow privacy while dressing and assessing overall perspectives of my frontage. Never content to let well enough alone, however, I'm compelled to sneak a peek at the posterior panorama as well.

Although my behind has not yet taken on lamp-table proportions, it cannot in any way be construed as my "best side."

Because the odds of successfully secluding myself from family members are comparable to Ed McMahon's appearing at my doorstep with megabuck check in hand, no sooner have I begun to choose my clothes, disrobe, and eyeball myself into a major blue funk than my children start pummeling the closet door.

One demands the immediate prosecution and punishment of a sibling rival; another alerts me to the fact that Fido just reCycled all over the kitchen floor; and a wee voice asks a can't-wait question such as "Where do stars go in the daytime, Mommy?"

Then, rather than wait an interminable forty-five seconds or so for me to come *out*, they burst *in* like a herd of crazed buffalo.

Due to the diminutive dimensions of the closet (and my pathetically slow reflexes), my nose and toes bear the brunt of these rude interruptions. As I totter around in the closet, there are no words, obscene or otherwise, to describe the sensation of feeling the skin atop my toes being peeled by the snaggled edge of a hollow-core door. And the only thing stopping said skin from being shucked all the way to my ankles is my nose, which has been simultaneously bashed to Pekinese proportions.

Whether the confrontation is literal or figurative, mirrors are like playground bullies: Avoiding them is impossible; there's no way I can *make* them be nice to me; and (despite what my mother always told me) ignoring them is easier said than done.

According to my encyclopedia, a glassblower named Bernard Perrot was responsible for developing a method to make smooth, reflective glass sheets—perfect for glazing, then gazing.

Oh, what a different world it would be had ol' Bernie put vanity aside and dedicated himself to inventing more user-*friendly* glassware like gunk-proof oven windows, and unsmudgable patio doors.

Juneau—My Kind of Town

By sifting through and carefully researching all available meteorologic data, I've decided to relocate my family to Juneau, Alaska.

That city's average daily temperature, June through August, is fifty-four degrees—a thermometer reading much too chilly for my kids' favorite summer pastime—swimming. Yep, that makes it *my* kind of town.

Granted, my view of backstroking the summer away has changed drastically thanks to the passage of years, the onset of cellulite, successive pregnancies, a sit-down career, and plenty of evidence that gravity is our enemy, not our friend.

As a child, I *lived* for those school's-out afternoons at the swimming pool, clad in a cartoon-charactered tank suit and diving for sunken penny treasures.

Now, I'm the Mom: the dry towel supplier, snack buyer, and shady-side lounge-lier who seems irresistible only to squadrons of sweat bees. And peeling my posterior from webbed chair straps has changed my perspective on birthdays and on what constitutes fun-in-the-sun.

But what really gets me where it hurts is the annual hope-springs-eternal search for a flattering swimsuit. According to fashion mavens, clothing of any kind should accentuate one's good features while diverting attention away from figure flaws. This advice seemed reasonable until I realized that my anatomical attributes were now limited to areas either above my eyebrows or below my knees.

Though bathing suits are cut from a yard of fabric or less and cover a third of my anatomy or less, I still expect those place-mat–sized garments to hold in, lift up, shift, and completely disguise all souvenirs of motherhood and my fondness for chocolate-covered everythings.

The department store's salestot (obviously born well after my bikini days ended) recommended a taut maillot with high, French-cut leg openings to visually slim my lumpish thighs. But after tugging the tight tank's shoulder straps in place, my drumsticks still rivaled Foghorn Leghorn's and the thought of trying to sit in that suit brought tears to my eyes.

A more matronly design featured a strip of gathered fabric sewn apron-style onto the waist area. This supposedly concealed midriff bulge and hyper hips, but to me, these bib-and-tuckered styles are like bed skirts: If I had nothing to hide I'd flaunt it, not flounce it.

To offset "Body Image Blues" and shape up for swimsuit season, health clubs staffed by Pecs "R" Us trainers guarantee a speedy return to youthful dimensions. But since I don't recall measuring up so well back then either, I see no reason to pay monthly fees so my appendages can be strapped to chrome-plated Veg-o-matic type machinery and pulverized into pubescent proportions.

So, instead of sucking in what remains of my abdominal musculature and trying to hide it behind a swatch of Spandex, I'm moving to Juneau—a kinder, gentler location.

And later, if I find out that Juneau isn't the answer, I've heard there's *no* place like Nome.

TWO

AN

Man: a creature

made at the end of the week's work

when God was tired.

—MARK TWAIN

Supermarketman

Though I consider my husband to be a Double-Stuff Oreo in the Cookie Jar of Life, I've learned from experience that sending him to the grocery store is like letting a two-year-old drink grape juice in the living room. In either case, I'll regret it.

Whether Himself is armed with a comprehensive supply list or simply winging it, he'll *forget* the one item I needed most, and *buy* approximately a hundred and fifteen others not written down or requested.

In the third grade, I was taught that the Four Basic Food Groups were Meat, Dairy, Vegetables and Fruits, and Grains and Legumes. If at least one representative of each group was not munched at every mealtime, my teacher swore, the onset of scurvy, beriberi, or rickets was just about inevitable.

That lecture cleaned a few cafeteria trays at my school for a while, but my husband must have been absent from class the week his homeroom studied the subject. As a result of this void in his educational background, he believes in the Four C's: Crunchy, Chewy, Carbonated, and Chocolate.

Granted, I've been known to lob boxes of ice cream bars or bags of nacho chips into the grocery cart myself. But when Supermarketman is in charge of procuring the provisions, his combination of cheddar puffs, caramel cubes, root beer, beef jerky strips, granola logs, and chocolate-covered cookies veers quite sharply off the prescribed path to proper nutrition.

After careening gleefully along Aisle 6's Snack Center, he rationalizes his goodie greed by searching elsewhere for bargains. *He* is the customer for whom all Day-Gloing "Reduced for Quick Clearance" and "Buy One Get One Free" signs were created.

I cannot argue that Hubby has saved our grocery budget a veritable fortune on keyless sardine cans, water-packed artichoke hearts, and a variety of expiring bakery items whose crusts are in need of a shave.

I *can* argue that pennies saved quickly become dollars wasted if family members would sooner graze on pasteurized fescue than swill a Supermarketman Supper Special: jalapeño pepper and liver pâté sandwiches.

Because Himself's curious collection of canned goods stays parked in the pantry, they eventually remind me of postpregnancy stretch marks: No matter how one attempts to disguise them, they just won't go away.

It might seem both logical and economical to simply ban Supermarketman from the grocery store, but on my list of most despised chores, food shopping is second only to picking chicken-bone fragments from the bowels of the garbage disposal.

Amazingly enough, Spouse actually *enjoys* steering a shopping cart with one welded wheel, mentally calculating the best buy between twelve-ounce cans of green beans marked two for one dollar and fourteen-ounce cans priced at fifty-two cents each, thunking melons for no known reason other than family tradition, not to mention scouting the shelves for items considered edible only by obscure South American Indian tribes.

Living with a Save-a-Fortune Cookie will never change my opinions pertaining to creating a proper nutritional balance, but it has redefined my idea of a "breadwinner."

Rather than the partner who earns the bigger paycheck, the "breadwinner" in my house is he who buys the supermarket's most outdated, mutilated, and leathery loaves for the *lowest* possible price.

Selective Hearing

George Washington's mother told him a hundred times not to cut down that cherry tree, but did he listen? Custer pooh-poohed his wife's advice on messing with those Indians. Mrs. Parker warned her daughter, "Nice boys don't rob banks," but Bonnie ran off with Clyde anyway.

As any wife and mother knows, husbands and children are experts at the art of Selective Hearing. In the animal world, this malfunction is comparable to the ostrich burying its head in the sand and believing itself invisible to predators. Fortunately, for most husbands and kids, mothers are seldom aggressively predatory . . . just frustrated.

When a woman marries, there's no mention of Selective Hearing in the "for better or for worse" and "in sickness and in health" parts of the ceremony she vows to take that man in spite of.

From that day forward, Hubby will always hear a friend whisper a Saturday afternoon tee time, your quiet confession to Mother that the grocery check bounced, or disparaging remarks detailing his character (or lack thereof) at frequencies previously detectable only by United States Navy radar. But he will *never* hear distinctly enunciated requests for milk or bread to be picked up on the way home, the sounds of toddlers being sick in the middle of the night in the middle of the living room carpet, teenagers arriving home two hours later than curfew, or the dog whining to go out. The same man who can hear his wallet being opened in another room is deaf to the thunder of an approaching garbage truck.

Once children come along, a mother realizes that they, too, can filter key words and phrases through their ears, and begin doing so at a surprisingly tender age.

Of course, Mother's auditory antennae can scan all familial frequencies, at all times, and without fail. From a spoon clinking against a bowl of "I-said-not-before-dinner" fudge ripple ice cream to an infant's quiet whimpers to hissed threats of impending sibling massacre, a mother's ear is never out of range. A house may be filled to the rafters with a dozen children and their father, but only Mother will hear and respond to the ringing telephone or buzzing doorbell.

Children *will* respond to certain words such as: *candy*, *cartoons*, *toy store*, *pepperoni pizza*, *swimming pool*, *yes*, *play*, and *go*. And if Mom has stashed the last box of chocolate mint Girl Scout cookies for her own well-deserved reward, any child over the age of five can hear and accurately identify the r-i-p of their wax-paper packaging, and appear at the scene with Olympic speed. Kids can hear Mom wearily running water for a desperately needed, take-me-away-please bubble bath, or paperback pages gently turning in the bathroom, and will scream an urgent need to use the toilet.

Teenagers hear checks being cashed at the bank, gas tanks filling at a self-service station, and new credit cards with higher user limits sliding into the mailbox.

Simultaneously, the words *lawn mower*, *homework*, *shut*, *clean*, *flush*, and *no* cannot be comprehended. And sentences beginning with "I want you to . . . ," "You can't . . . ," or "You already owe me . . ." don't register either.

Selective Hearing is the reason most mothers eventually become Yellers. They erroneously believe if the volume is raised, Spouse and children cannot deny hearing them. Though logical, this solution does not address the underlying problem and is akin to a chocoholic giving up broccoli as a weight-reduction technique.

Mom may holler up the stairs, from the porch, and through closed bedroom doors, and her turbocharged words will vibrate everything *but* the intended's eardrum. The neighbors will hear her, the mail carrier will hear her, the dog may leap up in terror, but her loved ones' lack of response only underscores a profound screech impediment.

Next, Mom will try a whisper campaign. Children pay attention to whispers because they think they are picking up the inside track on something they are absolutely *not* supposed to know about. Whispered instructions will still be "forgotten" or ignored, but at least this tactic relieves Old Yeller's chronic sore throat.

In desperation, mothers often resort to notes and charts. Although family members obviously have a hearing defect, they can *read*, can't they? A veritable flurry of little grocery lists appears for Dad, and notes alerting the kids to haircut and allergy appointments, requesting that underwear be changed, teeth be brushed and flossed, and that Fido be fed, are tucked into lunch boxes and briefcases—along with a few endearing missives to confuse the opposition.

In addition, a posterboard chore chart accompanied by a bag of gummed, shiny stars is magnetically attached to the refrigerator door. This duty roster not only assigns the jobs Mom's been jabbering about to the proper people, but also keeps tabs on their accomplishment.

Except soon, the wording of the notes will turn threatening, the chart will remain devoid of stars, the Shih Tzu will look like she's starving, and Dad's really sorry, but he forgot the milk again.

This is the moment when most mothers resign themselves to being seen but never heard. However, for those who stubbornly refuse to admit defeat, any library or bookstore has dozens of how-to volumes offering various foolproof formulas to encourage Spouse and children to share in the fulfillment of daily household responsibilities and upkeep.

Just don't get discouraged when you find them shelved in the Fiction section.

It's Simple, Sigmund

Dr. Sigmund Freud once queried, "What does a woman want?" To the best of my knowledge his question was never adequately answered, mostly because it's been mulled over by other males instead of being directed toward the gender more qualified to respond.

Some females might say their fondest desire lies in the acquisition of corporate chairs, unlimited income coupled with unlimited outgo, live-in household help, or the metabolism to wine and dine on whatever, whenever, without gaining an ounce. Granted, all those would be nice, but my personal preference is a much tougher scourge to purge.

To be blunt, all I want is for men to better understand Premenstrual Syndrome. Although PMS is no more gender-biased than prostate problems, men usually garner more sympathy for those once-in-a-lifetime plumbing malfunctions than we do for suffering approximately four hundred and twenty regularly scheduled periods of anatomical distress, discomfort, and downright misery.

Even if a woman is one of the fortunate few who escape the bloating, headaches, cramps, food cravings, overnight acne eruptions, fatigue, depression, and moodiness that manifest this affliction, she must still deal with a week of hygienic complications that can, at best, be described as "gross."

As a result, "I Enjoy Being a Girl" can be sincerely sung only twenty-one days a month. During the remaining seven, "It's My Party and I'll Cry If I Want to—You Would Cry Too if It Happened to You" is a more appropriate anthem.

I've often wondered if Eve had PMS when she taunted Adam with that apple. Perhaps the wily serpent promised her a cure for cramps if she made Adam munch a mouthful of that Edenistic fruit.

However, to be fair, possibly the males' historic inability to relate to us who writhe under PMS's influence comes from our own failure to adequately describe its symptoms.

The next time you awaken with your tummy pooched like a pumpkin, instead of wailing about your inability to zip your jeans, why not give your man a more graphic example of each internal terrorist attack.

To describe cramps, simply ask your mate to remove his shoe and sock. Have him firmly grasp his big toe in one hand and second toe with the other, then spread them apart as far as possible and hold that position for approximately four days. This demonstration should result in the immediate restocking of the medicine cabinet's aspirin supply—with the extra-strength brand.

Although we'd all enjoy a flashback to our youth, even a *man* knows that watching one's complexion turn into pepperoni pizza was *not* the kind of adolescent alchemy for which Ponce de Leon searched.

It's also a mite confusing for a husband to observe his wife refusing gooey desserts and midnight munchies for weeks, then find himself living with a one-woman feeding frenzy.

If Hubby still isn't getting the drift, explain your suddenly irrational behavior by reminding him of the time he purchased a four-hundred-dollar tool set to offset the cost of car repairs when it is well known he can't tell a dipstick from a distributor cap.

In my experience, the PMS-inspired peculiarity men complain about most is when normally even-tempered females alchemize into human nuclear reactors on the verge of meltdown. All too often, the male response to this periodic crabbiness is sneering, "Don't get your hormones in an uproar" or, "Yeah, I figured it was *that* time again."

Unfortunately, such snide remarks can shorten a man's life span quicker than playing Russian roulette—mostly because if his temporarily insane spouse draws a bead on him, she'll have made sure *all* the chambers are loaded.

So what's a man to do? Be patient, be kind, watch every blasted word you say and the tone with which you say it, and hide all sharp objects and blunt instruments normally found on the premises.

Oh, my dearly departed Sigmund, if only you'd been smart enough to ask a *woman* what a woman wants, you'd have been surprised at the simplicity of her answer.

No doubt, a more user-friendly set of internal organs would have topped the list.

Burnin' Daylight

I have nothing against mornings. Both sunrises I've personally witnessed were no less than spectacular, and although A.M. television talk shows are equally as inane as their P.M. counterparts, I'll admit, early birds *can* keep abreast of the day's projected high temperatures in Reykjavik, Iceland, and the Chicago Livestock Exchange's current feeder-pig prices.

However, as Spouse habitually bounces out of bed at 6:00 A.M., he expects me to do likewise. But because I only retired about four hours earlier, I usually respond to reveille with snarled remarks that question whether his parents were holy-wedlocked on the day of his birth.

Granted, we supposedly douse our bedside lamps simultaneously, but while I've spent the evening on frivolities like school lunch preparation, bill paying, helping with homework, doing housework, or refereeing sibling rivalries, he's been snoozing with one hand tucked under his head and the other death-gripping the television's remote control. Later, when that rested Romeo awakens rarin' for romance, he just can*not* figure out why his Juliet is dead on her feet.

Although reasonably insightful others would credit Spouse with lengthy head starts on his daily sleep requirement, *he* doesn't see it that way. In his estimation, since these nightly naps are taken while fully dressed and lying on *top* of the bedcovers, they don't "count." Therefore, come morning, he feels perfectly justified in slapping my haunches playfully and crowing, "You're burnin' daylight! Time to rise and shine!"

Suffice it to say, my thoughts at those moments center on

the "until death do us part" portion of our marriage vows. While I have stayed steadfast and true to those "for better, for worse, for richer, and for poorer" promises, I swear, the minister never said a *word* about showing up for breakfast.

Once I'm awake and have pretty much decided to remain that way, the first thing I want is a cup of hot, black coffee. The last thing I want is several pairs of childish eyes watching me drink it. And *I* enjoy sitting tableside while they cannibalize corn puffs and sugar-frosted zoo creatures about as much as *they* enjoy my remarks on Daughter's overdone eye makeup, Younger Son's twice-worn shirt, and the suspicious lump bulging Other Daughter's backpack.

Worse yet, despite friends' and neighbors' awareness of my nocturnal nature, some have the audacity to call at ungodly hours like 8:30 A.M.

When I moan into the phone a greeting that's most of "Hello," they'll respond with a self-righteous "My goodness! Did I wake you *up*?" as if that concept is as foreign to them as quantum physics.

At that point, I have only three options:

- Attempt a combination bald-faced lie and sympathy plea by coughing a few times, then wheezing, "No, I've got a

touch of cold/sinus infection/flu/bubonic plague that's making my voice sound funny."

• Adopt an answering-machine monotone and say, "Sorry, I can't come to the phone right now. Please leave your name and number and I'll get back to you as soon as possible."

• Admit that yes, I was snoozing, and therefore must undoubtedly be the laziest wench ever born between the shores of the U. S. of A.

Honestly, all this lifelong night owl wants is some "Variety is the spice of life" understanding. Just because my bedtime usually falls well after the witching hour, doesn't mean I'm flawed. But it *does* mean I'll be a real witch if I'm awakened too soon by a nauseatingly cheerful husband or neighbor.

At least I know Spouse and I aren't the first rooster/owl combo to suffer through sleep differences. In fact, I feel certain that one dark and stormy night a couple of hundred years ago, Ben Franklin chirped to his wife, for the 34,678th time, "Early to bed, early to rise, makes a man healthy, wealthy, and wise, dear."

And that's when Mrs. Franklin told him to go tie a key to a kite and fly it.

"E" Is for "Exasperation"

My marriage, like most, depends on mature levels of negotiation and compassionate arbitration. If Spouse insists on keeping our home's thermostat at Siberian settings, he can't complain about my sleeping in sweat suits. If I spend countless seconds slaving over a hot microwave, zapping delicious, home-nuked meals, the least he can do is load the dishwasher after dinner.

Yet there is one area of Our Life Together that continues to defy compromise: *I* say the big red "E" on our car's gasoline gauge warns of an almost empty fuel tank, but to Spouse, it stands for "Enough."

Whether our planned excursion is a short trip to the supermarket or a tour of these great United States, despite my remarks that the needle is rapidly sinking into the "E," Himself always assures me we have *enough* gasoline to get there.

He then offers proof of this extremely optimistic opinion by stating the capacity of the tank, then multiplying the guesstimated amount of gasoline remaining times the car's advertised miles-per-gallon ratio. An additional fifty miles is added to *that* sum to include the ungauged two tablespoonfuls trickling through the fuel lines.

Later, when the bone-dry engine sputters to a halt along the shoulder of a high-speed freeway, the wind-shearing sensation created by passing semis will temporarily entertain the kids in the backseat. However, the nearest service station is seldom less than three miles back from whence we came, and Spouse has never set a land-speed record in his life.

Just after he disappears over the horizon in search of a petroleum-products emporium, at least one child will cry, "I gotta go potty—NOW!"

As I scan the surrounding, closely mown landscape, invariably barren of any concealing shrubbery or rock formations, the child will "accidentally" relieve herself all over the upholstery and my in-case-it-gets-chilly jacket—giving a more literal interpretation to the term "carpool."

Before Mr. MPG returns, all the gum, restaurant mints, and aspirin stashed in my purse and the glove compartment have been consumed, one hundred and sixty-seven rounds of license-plate bingo have been played, a hundred and twenty-three incidents of "*He keeps touching me*!" have been refereed, and I am seriously considering throwing myself in front of an oncoming UPS truck.

When the car is finally reoctaned and ready to roll, the children wisely exercise their right to remain silent. Because Spouse already knows *my* answer to the "How in the devil could we have run out of gas?" question, he proceeds to discuss the dilemma with a more objective party: the dashboard.

Although a lengthy recitation of grumbles and gripes follows, the accuracy of his earlier mathematical wizardry is never in dispute. Instead, he insists the fault lies with:

- An inaccurate gauge (the "They just don't build them like they used to" approach).
- The manufacturer's mileage statistics (the "Somebody should sue them for false advertising" edict).
- The weight of *my* belongings in the trunk (not his golf bag, tool box, and enough fishing tackle to land Moby Dick) generated too much "drag" and befouled his bottom line.

I've read that automotive engineers are close to perfecting an electric-engined vehicle. Not only will this invention lessen our nation's dependency on fossil fuel, the first time my Old Fossil forgets to kilowatt the car, he'll learn his lesson.

After all, lugging liters of premium unleaded over hills and through dales is one thing. Going the distance dragging a 15,840-foot extension cord is quite another.

Spousework

Surveys have revealed that most husbands still do less than their fair fifty-percent share of the housework.

Happily, Spouse does contribute to the cleaning, except he takes his half out of each *task*, instead of the *total*. And he rarely does even those duties in a manner made famous by Frank Sinatra: "My Way."

For example, due to the dimensions of our home's cabinets, Spouse has used a trifolded bath towel every morning since about the mid-seventies. Nevertheless, he invariably folds loads of clean linens into *quarters*, then tries to cram the stack of too-big terries into the small space provided. Because tugging the topmost towel causes all of them to fall to the floor, and I'm the only one who ever notices those heaps, it's become *my* job to threefold and reshelve.

Spouse knows where they belong, knows my bureau isn't booby-trapped, and knows I've drawered approximately 89,341 pairs of his underwear, but he always parks *my* panties on top of the dresser. Not only does this tawdry display detract from the room's overall decor, but if I wanted to flaunt my finery, I'd put it on last when I dressed, instead of first.

Our kitchen is equipped with an automatic dishwasher guaranteed to blast off meal messes and milk rings, yet when Spouse has dish duty, he *prerinses* everything to squeaky cleanliness—a quirk I consider comparable to preheating a microwave oven.

As gallons of wasted water gurgle down the drain, Spouse is arranging three juice glasses, a couple of coffee mugs, a pair of plates, a saucepan, six cereal bowls, and a handful of flatwear into a can't-hold-another-teaspoon-sized load.

Of course, if any of the aforementioned are made of plastic, they're pronged on the bottom rack nearest the heat coil, which accounts for our curious collection of oval-rimmed tumblers, scallop-handled spatulas, and trapezoided Tupperware.

While we own both an upright and a canister-model vacuum cleaner, Spouse prefers the latter because its brush attachment *de*taches. Rather than stoop and manhandle carpet clutter like peanut shells, single socks, wadded tissues, abandoned lock blocks, and pizza crusts, he pops off the aforementioned attachment and sucks everything smaller than the sofa up the open hose.

When it comes to dusting, Spouse's style is an all-or-under-nothing proposition. Either he oils everything from ashtrays to the Zenith's screen (your basic lemon-scented lube job) or he rags *around* all table-topped accessories.

Granted, those all-out efforts definitely leave a shine behind, but the latter leaves guests wondering whether the Dust Fairy lives under our lamps.

Like most couples, our house *getting* was relatively easy. It's going halvsies on the house*keeping* that's posed some problems. It's taken me awhile, but I'm finally figuring out that sharing domestic drudgery requires a special kind of guy who forsakes all druthers, and'll do windows, too.

And a special kind of gal who can keep her mouth shut and let him do it . . . *his* way.

When the Whatchamacallit Won't

Whenever I report that a mechanical object is malfunctioning or making a "funny" noise, I get the third degree from Spouse. Rather than take my word for it, I must prove to him, by a preponderance of evidence, that the doohickey doesn't, the thingamajig's jammed, or the whatchamacallit won't.

Naturally, all the above gizmos function perfectly during these demonstrations because the natural enemy of any species of gadgetry is a fella armed with screwdrivers, hammers, and Vise-grip pliers.

Thanks to this man-and-machinery conspiracy, I recently whiled away an entire afternoon in the Great Outdoors. Although I'd mentioned that our front door was developing a persnickety streak, as usual I failed to make my case—he found the accused "not guilty."

And the very next day, during an innocent traipse to the mailbox, that steel-shielded, guaranteed burglar-resistant slab of security slammed and dead-bolted behind me.

There are few things more humbling than being on the outside, looking in to your own home. And few moves more desperate than thumbing the bell, knowing full well there's nary a soul inside but a couple of gerbils and a goldfish.

My children leave the basement door open often enough that an occasional raking of the family room is necessary, but when I needed their carelessness the most, the back entrance was sealed tighter than Tut's tomb. And the passage custom-cut for an eight-pound miniature dachshund proved slightly shy, dimensionally, for an average-sized human homeowner.

And I suppose I should be thrilled that our expensive, thief-proof window latches can withstand the most determined assaults perpetrated by a woman wielding twigs, various barbecue utensils, and discarded Superhero weaponry.

While waiting for a key-carrying teen's arrival from school, I decided the next time the youngsters needed disciplining, I wouldn't send them to their fun-and-games-equipped bedrooms. They'll be banished to the front porch where there's absolutely nothing to do but pet the dog, read and reread the junk mail, and listen to the telephone ring and ring and ring.

Granted, I also jiggled the doorknob repeatedly as if it would voluntarily relent, reflected nostalgically on the good old days when backyards had outhouses, and pondered whether our insurance agent would consider a brick hurled through the nearest window an Act of God.

Mr. Fixit's reaction to my tale of woe was akin to one watching a Three Stooges film festival. Amid a disgustingly lengthy series of chortles, he said, "Why didn't you call me at the office? I'd have come home and let you in"—common sense on a par with inquiring of a pedestrian just keelhauled by a speeding furniture truck, "Gosh, are you hurt?"

To prove my point, four hundred and thirty-eight "test shuts" followed, ranging from plaster-rattling slams to the gentlest of closures. I even tried putting a little prerelease "English" on the doorknob. All failed miserably in making the dead-bolt slide home by itself, but succeeded in giving Spouse many more mirthful moments.

But, as he should have known, he who laughs last . . .

A few nights later, clad only in his underwear, Spouse grumped outside to quiet our howling hound. Fiendishly, the front door creaked to a close behind him and the bolt whapped solidly in place.

Speaking from experience, time does pass slowly when one is stranded on the porch, but despite what Spouse says, I swear, it only took me five—ten minutes, tops, to "Unlock the @#$%&*#$%@ door!"

Shoot, it didn't take him much longer than that to fix the @#$%&*#$%@ lock, either.

'Tis the Season

After much calendar consultation, it was clear that December thirteenth was the *only* day everyone in the family was available for our traditional Putting Up the Christmas Tree. Naturally, when that day dawned, the projected high temperature matched my shoe size, and an "unseasonable" combination of snow, sleet, and freezing rain was pelting in via Siberia.

The children *did* chime in on choruses of "I'm Dreaming of a White Christmas" en route to an evergreen emporium established seasonally on a supermarket parking lot, but once we arrived, they made it clear they had absolutely no intention of abandoning our toasty van for a wintry wonderland.

Since tree lots don't have drive-through window service, and Spouse and I learned years ago that forcing our children's participation makes shopping for anything about as much fun as a group root canal, just Ourselves, without the elves, entered the chain-sawed forest.

Immediately, Spouse drifted over to what I call the "shrub section." With a couple more years' growth and some serious fertilizing, the saplings huddled there might have a future as landscape plantings.

While stooping to show off his favorite, Spouse tried convincing me that after screwing its scrawny trunk into the tree stand, its topknot just might knock the nubs off our living room's sixteen-foot ceiling.

Because I could have carried the sprout home in my handbag, I realized his illusion of grandeur had a lot more to do with these trees' per-foot pricing than with our ownership of the world's tallest Christmas tree holder.

To counter his Scrooginess, I set my sights on Mother Nature's firstborn: a majestic mountain of fir capable of cuddling a flotilla of angels crafted from Ivory Liquid bottles and a herd of clothespin Rudolphs, *and* providing about eleven ricks of postseason firewood.

Scrooge snidely said *my* towering tannenbaum would require flatbed truck delivery, the enlargement of our front entry to barnlike dimensions, and the jacking of several ceiling joists in the living room. Well, I told *him* precisely where he could put the aforementioned truck, double doors, and rafters. Then "we" compromised on an eight-footer with a built-in "wall" side.

Attaching Tree to stand should be a simple task, except it never is. Tree's trunk is always too fat to fit the holder, which means shaving it down to size *with* the edge of an ax blade, and *without* amputating any fingers or toes.

Once tapered as precisely as a #2 pencil point and bolted securely into the stand, we found, setting it upright, that:

- Pine sap is one of the world's stickiest substances and does not wash off—only wears off,
- Not only was Tree's trunk chubby, we hadn't noticed it was curvier than a strip of crisp bacon.
- Because it was accustomed to a natural environment, Tree felt compelled to molt a few million needles to lend its new home a more outdoorsy ambience.

While the elves raked the rug, Spouse and I cornered Tree and corrected its chronic leftward lean by shimming the short side with last year's telephone book. That added a tad more elevation than needed, so a magazine was shoved under a second leg, and consequently, two coasters were wedged beneath the third. A precautionary guy wire strung from trunk to yonder bookcase ensured Tree's upright posture.

Last year, like every year preceding, I promised myself I'd wind our multitudinous strings of Taiwanese Twinklers around their holders before packing them away. I remembered that heartfelt vow when I gazed upon an electrical tumbleweed of monstrous proportions.

Within minutes, the floor was a veritable minefield of dislodged bulbs and trip wires and the grumbling untanglers were actively engaged in hissing obscenities, practicing noose-making and handcuffing skills, and wrapping Little Brother with the untangled cords and plugging him in.

Quite proudly they declared they had not only figured out a great way to simultaneously test the strings and prevent their retangling, they had accidentally discovered a terrific costume idea for next Halloween.

Naturally, the only functional flickerers we salvaged were the kind with a plug at only one end, so the cords had to be fanned out from a central socket like spokes on a wheel. A handful of twisty ties, three extension cords, and two trips to the breaker box were needed before a well-balanced lighting scheme (and potential fire hazard) was created.

The children's enthusiasm for further Tree trimming had waned by now, so to speed up the process, they adorned only the middling branches with about fifty-seven ornaments each—an effect I called the "Star-Spangled Belt Look."

At that moment, neither Peace on Earth nor Joy to the World seemed particularly doable, but jingling a few bells sounded like a darned good idea.

However, a speech entitled "I Try So Hard to Make Christmas Special and This Is the Thanks I Get" was equally effective. In a flash, the smaller son scrambled up the ladder to hang 'em high, the six-foot-fiver sprawled on the carpet for bottom branch beautification, and the girls were arguing *who* was better qualified to hang *what, where.*

Yes, 'tis the season for miracles. Eventually, the children were tucked all snugly in their beds, with visions of exorbitantly priced merchandise dancing in their heads. Tree was twinkling merrily; its branches heavy-laden with family memories and treasures, hung with loving care instead of haste.

I say the same thing every year, but every year it's true—our angel-crowned, popcorn-garlanded symbol of the season is the most beautiful one we've *ever* had. And you never know . . . ol' Santa Spouse just might spring for a *nine*-footer next year!

Oh Say Can't You See?

It never ceases to amaze me how selectively observant the menfolk in my family are. Younger Son is forever asking me where this or that toy is—as if I while away the day target-practicing with his X-57 SuperSonic Big Buddy Bazooka, then hide the evidence beneath the sofa cushions.

Of course if I did, his arsenal would be lost for all eternity. Be it weaponry or a part of his wardrobe, he insists he "didn't see it" lying smack in the middle of the hallway, although he's been walking around it all day.

The boy *does* have an unerring eye for spying boxes of cupcakes stashed behind the pantry's veritable fortress of canned vegetables. But an ink stain the size of Argentina splotching a leg of his good jeans? Never saw it before, and his expression is darn near an accusation that *I* tampered with his trousers just to get him in trouble.

Older Son's specialty is not noticing the smoke from cremated pizzas billowing out of the oven. When borrowing my car, the fact that the gas gauge's "F" has descended to a solid "E" always comes as a total surprise to the lad whose last eye examination yielded a twenty-twenty score.

Typical oversights also include muddy trailings of size 13 sneakers crudding across the carpeting, any clock's numerical hint that curfew is near (let alone passed), and notes from his mother listing chores to be done.

But with Supermanlike X-ray capabilities, Elder Son can scope a twenty-dollar bill in my wallet even if it's sandwiched between a dry cleaner's receipt and a grocery list. And the time I accidentally nudged the merest, most *inconsequential* ding in *his* car door? He zeroed in on *that* bitsy blemish from no less than fifty paces.

Yet, the boys are hardly to blame for their selective sightedness. They learned it at the knee of the master: their father.

August to January, while focused intently on the tube, the man hasn't missed a single, unflagged offsides committed by any National or American Football League lineman, since 1976.

But around the house, we've affectionately nicknamed him "Old Leadeye," because he constantly accuses me of hiding his favorite shirt, when, of course, the rag is hanging in plain sight on the closet rod.

Then there's all those accumulated trash bags heaped on the kitchen floor. Old Leadeye can mosey among them for days, but when I pointedly remark on their presence, he looks astonished, as if I just tweaked my nose and conjured them on the spot.

Whether it's mayonnaise jars virtually waving their little lids off *right there* in the front of the refrigerator, car keys gleaming *right there* on the dresser, or any one of the 2,578,947 *right there* items with which I fill his blank after, "Have you seen the ———," I'm convinced Spouse wouldn't spot a herd of water buffalo grazing in our front yard.

To prove my point, a few days ago I completely rearranged the living room furniture, hung new curtains, cornered a banana palm big enough for Cheetah to homestead in, and cleaned everything from the cobwebbed ceiling to the crumby carpet.

When Old Leadeye got home, I even helped by hinting, "Do you notice anything different?"

Obviously perplexed, he turned and slowly surveyed the room. I watched as he looked up, glanced down, peered all around. Then his eyes met mine, and locked.

Grinning ear-to-ear, and with a note of triumph in his voice, he said, "I sure *do*! You got your hair cut, didn't you?"

THREE

HOUSEWORK

There is no need to do any housework at all.

After the first four years,

the dirt doesn't get any worse.

—*Quentin Crisp*

Futility Room

Because average home prices have risen to levels equaling the gross national products of several minor European provinces, contractors have added a dash of high-tech spiciness to garnish their salable offerings.

This is why bathrooms have become "Home Spas," kitchens, "Food Preparation Centers," living rooms are "Great Rooms" (even if merely mediocre), and wherever a television blares unattended is advertised as a "Media Room."

Considering the number of years I've dwelled in a heavily mortgaged American Dream, I think it only fair that *I* be allowed to rename a room, too. But since so many have already been altered, I'm left with few candidates for conversion.

Baptizing the master bedroom the "Boudoir" sounded as though I was talking with a mouth full of peanut butter and besides, it's been done. As Spouse and I have four children, perhaps the "Creativity Center" would be more appropriate, but might encourage the impression that a *fifth* is at all conceivable. "Slumber Chamber" paints the mental image of a soundproofed room, which no cubic inch of our home is, and "The Bear's Den" was viewed by my husband as a critique of his morning personality which was, I admit, my source of inspiration.

I finally surrendered the idea of trademarking rooms I share with other family members and focused my attention on the one space my family has granted me full ownership of: the utility room.

Though the first descriptive titles that came to mind

couldn't be repeated in the presence of impressionable children, it was simple to devise a more appropriate name for this basemented bastion. The change required only the addition of the letter "F," and it definitely describes my attitude when crossing that lint-bunnied threshold.

From this day forward, the "Garment Recycling Center" will be known to me as The Futility Room.

In my extremely experienced opinion, "laundry" and "futility" should be synonymous anyway, because laundry is akin to an eighth-grader's homework assignments: seldom, if ever, completely finished.

As any futility-room executive will agree, no sooner have nine loads been sudsed, rinsed, softened, spun, dried, and folded than a collection of muddied sports uniforms, playtime ensembles worn for a maximum of thirteen and a half minutes, and a bundle of bedsheets that haven't been changed since the Bush administration rumble down the chute and land limply upon the linoleum.

Unending supply is depressing enough, but it seems that if left alone in a darkened futility room, laundry can reproduce itself faster than a hamster's harem. If I mistakenly abandon a few towels for the next day's load, overnight an entire litter of nocturnally spawned washcloths, hand towels, bath towels, and beach towels are born in my absence. Then, disturbed by the terrycloth nymphomaniacs' mating ritual, the detergent carton spits up a few granulated ounces on the floor—a sort of "moon affecting the Tide" phenomenon.

Posting "No Trespassing" signs on the clothing chute's trapdoor, threatening to will my lifetime collection of 2,719 unmatched socks to their original owners, transferring soap supplies to lidded containers, and leaving the ceiling light on all night in hopes the linens will behave haven't helped, so I feel I should at *least* be extended the honor of renaming my temple of gloom The Futility Room.

Of course, I realize changing names to better reflect actual characteristics *must* be limited to domestic living spaces. Otherwise, I'd be tempted to rechristen my children: Sleepy, Grumpy, Droopy, and Whoops.

Gimme a Hint, Heloise

Dear Heloise,

I've been a fan of yours for many years. I regularly read your newspaper column, own several of your how-to books, and really try to do as you say. However, doing as I do often creates some cleaning quandaries I haven't seen addressed in your writings.

For instance, is there a hands-off method to remove doggy droppings from the bottoms of my son's tennis shoes that will not induce nausea or aggravate my sinus condition?

My youngest has an unequaled talent for trampling turf taffy wherever it may lurk. My policy to let heaping dog dookies lie is not very efficient because the stacks of polluted Pumas are rising and replacement footwear costs are escalating proportionately.

For another thing, although I've tried all adhesives advertised as strong and effective, I've yet to find one strong enough to repair a shattered platter.

Silly me, I accidentally hurled the heirloom (a gift from my mother-in-law) in the direction of my true love's head. I can happily report it missed *him*, but secondary impact with the fireplace wall "chipped" the piece quite severely.

My mother-in-law is coming to visit next month and I fully expect her to inquire of the plate's whereabouts approximately two minutes after her arrival. I doubt if showing her a sackful of shards will do much to cement our relationship.

And my car's backseat has a nagging odor for which I

welcome a remedy. Recently, I volunteered to chauffeur a few of my daughter's classmates to a school-sponsored Day at the Fair.

Suffice it to say, all those grape-flavored snow cones, cotton-candy clouds, and spicy sausages committed a gravity-defying act during the winding drive home. Now, each time I park my car in a sunny locale I'm reminded of this quality-timed parenting event. What can I do to clear the air?

Laundry is one of my most trying household hurdles. I use your hints regularly for successfully removing blood, grass, and grease stains, but my husband created an unusual cleaning conundrum I've yet to resolve.

After much scrimping and saving, I bought him a new golf shirt and matching shorts for his birthday. Naturally, this was the ensemble he wore while pouring our concrete patio extension.

Can you imagine my reaction (see reference to platter above) when I saw those pricey duds completely speckled by cement splatters? Even the pocketed reptile's tiny torso was suffocating beneath a glob of gray goo. Can you help?

I'll certainly appreciate any wisdom you can impart on my behalf. After all, if the Guru of Grime cannot assist me in my hour of need, who can?

Sincerely yours,
A grateful reader

P.S. Please note: I've enclosed an overnight mailer to speed your reply. My mother-in-law just telephoned (collect, of course) to say she'll arrive much sooner than expected. At the very least, healing that hashed Haviland must commence immediately!

Superfridge

What has as many as four doors, a Lighted Diagnostic Display Control Panel, comes in several designer colors with shiny chrome trim, and can call its own repairperson?

Answer: a "Domestic Nutrition Storage Center." Which used to be called a refrigerator.

These new high-tech marvels look like giant computers with handles. They not only chill the groceries and manufacture ice cubes, but are also considered decorator items for the Primary Meal Preparation Center (formerly known as the kitchen).

Listening to the salesperson's description of all the new features available only made me wonder what sort of childless Fridge Frankenstein devised these incredible hulks.

For instance, some models have a built-in wine chiller to provide "a perfectly cooled liquid accompaniment to your next intimate dinner for two."

But my husband and I have four children. When we sit down for an intimate dinner for two, we bask in the romantic glow of twin golden arches, and make the kids unwrap *their* entrees at a separate table.

"A sparkling chilled water dispenser is conveniently located outside the door." Translation: My youngest and all his buddies will be constantly in the kitchen shoving on the water stirrup, instead of drinking refreshingly lukewarm hose water as children have done for generations.

"An interior lazy Susan for handy condiment storage" is another available option. Jimmy the Greek could tout Las Vegas odds that my four will be placing their bets on who can spin the shelf fastest and make the mayonnaise jar fly farthest—best two-out-of-three wins.

The Lighted Diagnostic Display Control Panel supposedly alerts the homeowner when the power has been interrupted, when the door is ajar, when a fresh batch of ice cubes is ready; it can even signal when a service call is needed. Doesn't that sound ingenious? Stop and think about it.

In my home, the refrigerator door is *always* open, propped by a teenager who is being simultaneously frostbitten by the cold and tanned by the interior light bulb.

Who *cares* when a fresh batch of ice has been ejected into the bin? What am I supposed to do—dig the "stale" cubes from underneath and toss them into the sink? Worrying about serving old ice to my guests doesn't exactly keep me pacing the floor at night.

And honestly, do you want an appliance to tell you when it wants the immediate attention of a fifty-dollar-per-hour (plus mileage) repairperson? What if it's only faking illness like a fourth-grader on history exam day? I'll stick to my own traditional barometer of appliance health, thank you—if it doesn't work, I'll have it fixed.

I've saved my favorite invention for last: a roll-out shelf for two-liter soda bottles. Did anyone consider the effects of *gravity* when assembling this? Each time a child racks a jug of pop on this little wonder, mothers all over America will sing,

Flow gently sweet cola, your lid's not on tight.
Flow gently grape fizzy, on your side all last night.

Certainly I give credit to the engineers and designers who are diligently developing new ideas to fit the ever-changing needs and lifestyles of the appliance-buying public. I understand and salute their attempts to make something as mundane as the family refrigerator into a more exciting product.

But all I want is a tall metal box that'll keep the ice cream frozen, hold five gallons of milk and one hundred and nine plastic butter bowls full of suspicious-looking leftovers, and not boss me around.

Kiddie Litter

I live with the Three Little Pigs, but this story is no fairy tale.

Let me better illustrate my domestic conditions: I share a two-and-a-half-story home with one husband, four children (two girls, two boys), a miniature dachshund named Thumper, three cats, Sharky the bird, John Wayne gerbil, guinea pigs (an exact population count varies from moon phase to moon phase), assorted tropical fish, and Leon the chameleon.

Hubby (The Big Bad Wolf) and I have tried to be good parents and set an example worthy of our children's imitation, partially because we are outnumbered. Our offspring are all potty-trained, usually eat with silverware, and have been heard on occasion to mumble "Please" and "Thank you," especially if the request involves major sums of money or keys to an automobile.

But we have only managed to instill the time-honored axiom "Cleanliness is next to godliness" in Older Daughter's mind. Younger Daughter, as well as Big and Little Sons, are in a "root hog or die" contest of wills. And if they don't start cleaning their rooms pretty soon, they'll all be stricken as beneficiaries in mine.

For years we've cajoled, pleaded, bribed—even threatened bodily harm—to this trio who contentedly occupy their custom-created hovels. I'll admit, the boys have suffered a greater share of our wrath because their indoor landfill is directly across the hall from our own comely quarters and the resulting traffic route forces us to pass (and smell) their "sty" several times per day.

Younger Daughter's room, however, is upstairs and a few steps from her neater sister's domain, with an often grungy and grudgingly shared bathroom demilitarizing the zone between. Because these are the only rooms on the second floor, I have no compelling urge to visit unless I'm retrieving a truckload or so of my "borrowed" personal possessions. After all, when there's just cause for a hypertensive seizure on the main floor, why take any chances and venture upstairs?

Ignoring the situation improved my attitude, but didn't solve the problem. When our home's resale value started dropping appreciably, a more permanent solution had to be found. Nagging didn't work. Shutting the doors didn't either because they never stayed shut. And grounding a child within the limits of a bedroom equipped with computers, televisions, stereos, and telephones was more a privilege of privacy than a punishment.

I briefly considered banishing the boys to the basement, but neither son felt entirely comfortable living in subterranean darkness. Besides, I quickly realized this maneuver would only spread the slobs *all over* the house.

Desperation must be the mother of invention because one day I was struck by an idea that bordered on genius. Instead of keeping the tidy Older Daughter sequestered invisibly upstairs to contrast with, or possibly inspire, her sloppy sister, and the boys downstairs with their monumental mess assaulting at least three of our senses daily, why not transfer the good housekeeper down to our level and beam up the boys?

Granted, the upper rooms would suffer total devastation on a par with London after the Blitz, but at least my three little pigs would be penned up together!

Each victim had to be approached in just the right manner, and I started my motivational campaign with First Daughter.

"Accentuate the positive," I silently reminded myself, then began by outlining the basic idea, sprinkling in perks like the fact her new location was several steps closer to the telephone, and that she'd no longer share a bathroom with a sibling who has never hung up a wet towel, capped a toothpaste tube, or bought her own makeup in her life. No sweat. One down, two to go.

After snuggling my next candidate on my lap, I spun a tale worthy of his seven-year-old imagination. There were adventures to behold if he moved upstairs. He could see his best buddy's house from the window, and build forts from sheets and blankets to his heart's content with no protest from me. A promotion to official School Bus Spotter was offered as incentive. The clincher was a promise that Daddy would build shelves especially for Son's dinosaur collection. Never mind that the promise was initiated without the carpenter's knowledge or consent—Younger Son jumped up and got packing.

But those two victories were merely shadowboxing bouts before the main event. Thirteen-year-old boys aren't easily convinced of anything, so I decided to confuse Big Son with honesty—I said I had some good news and some bad news and I didn't bother letting him pick which he wanted to hear first.

The good news: He was moving upstairs where the room was larger, the walls relatively unscarred, and where he would be out of our sight before we were out of our minds. The bad news? He was still stuck sharing quarters with Little Brother, but I would separate the bunk beds so he no longer had to sleep with one knee wedged against the ceiling.

In addition, one whole wall of his new room could be dedicated exclusively to his beloved collection of Oklahoma Sooners' football memorabilia *if* his *Sports Illustrated* Swimsuit Editions were stashed in his underwear drawer where they belonged. When Older Son's enthusiasm escalated to that of a professional pallbearer's, I knew I had him.

Needless to say, the quality of life at our house has improved dramatically. Today, as I passed Older Daughter's door, I whiffed the sweet scent of gardenia perfume instead of choking on filthy sweat sock fumes.

I ascended the stairs to check on Young Son and found him contentedly knee-deep in all the prehistoric paraphernalia he was supposed to stow on the new shelves.

On Elder Son's yonder wall, the OU football team, en masse, surrounds a carefully lettered sign that threatens "IF YOU TOUCH ANY OF MY STUFF I'LL KILL YOU." (Too bad the brother it's intended for can't read most of the words.)

I move down the hallway and through the haze defining Younger Daughter's personal space, but ignore the implied invitation symbolized by her open door. More than likely, there's just so much stuff piled in front of it that it's impossible *to* shut.

I may have won the battle only to lose the war, but parents have got to give a little to get a little. Besides, after the kids are grown and gone, it shouldn't cost too much to simply slice *off* the second floor, should it?

Multiple Organize-'ems

Like most working women, I clean out the refrigerator whenever I forget to buy Fido food. Taking out the ironing board is limited to emergencies and national holidays. And a well-aimed lawn sprinkler doesn't spit-and-polish the windows, but it will rinse off the dust and dead bugs.

One day, however, I noticed spiders were building time-share condos in every corner of the ceiling. Dust bunnies the size of Harvey lurked beneath every bed. Fingerprints in the hallways looked like growth charts, with smudges above the doors marking rites of passage.

Two things were certain: (1) Something had to be done to get our house in order; (2) I hadn't made most of the messes and I sure as Heloise wasn't going to clean them all, either.

Because Spouse was already doing his share of the dirty work, I encouraged our children's assistance by first disproving their belief that all housework is a direct violation of the Child Labor Act, and second, by offering bribes. Unfortunately, my plan backfired because those who happily inhabit bedrooms resembling toxic waste dumps are rarely the best candidates for a cleaning crew.

So, I sought professional help. After telephoning a few housekeeping services I was astounded to discover that physicians and dusticians charge approximately the same rates for house calls.

Remembering the gist of my "By God, If You Want Something Done Right Around Here You'd by God Better Do It

Yourself, by God," speech, I went to the supermarket to load up on seventy-nine dollars' worth of skull-and-crossboned chemicals guaranteed to clean without scrubbing, shine without buffing, repel dust and mildew, and remove purple soft-drink stains from beige carpeting. While waiting in the checkout line, I noticed the words, "TEN EASY WAYS TO CLEAN & ORGANIZE YOUR HOME" screaming from a magazine cover.

The article's author, Wanda Whiteglove, was heralded as a "home management expert" who believed *organization* the key to a constantly clean home.

Since my résumé lists "organizational skills" just above "does small engine repair," Wanda seemed just the savior I needed to help me take a bite out of grime.

Her first crusade against clutter recommended the purchase of *filing cabinets.* Then, everything from sales receipts and appliance warranties accumulated since matrimony, to scads of crayoned keepsakes lugged home daily by the backpack load, should be placed in labeled manila folders and filed alphabetically in the drawers.

This was certainly more ingenious than chucking papers into the junk drawer and sifting occasionally in panic, but after scouting possible sites in my home to store this domestic data base, I only found one place large enough to accommodate it. And Spouse refused to share the shower stall with a four-drawered paper holder.

The next strategy stressed *scheduling* as a cure for drudgery. According to some artistically drawn diagrams, Mondays, Wednesdays, and Fridays should be dedicated to vacuuming, dusting, and doing laundry. Tuesdays and Thursdays: sandblasting bathrooms, ironing, mopping, and peeling bed linens. Saturdays, devotionals were for sprucing our not-so-great outdoors, and Sundays were to be reserved for miscellaneous maintenance: i.e., all chores left undone during the preceding six.

Wanda Whiteglove's calendar calisthenics did seem scientific, but she made one b-i-g assumption: that I wanted to spend the *entire week* cleaning my house.

Discouraged but not defeated, I skimmed ahead to the section on *kitchens.* Logically, any room devoted to cookery would be much more orderly if it only stored groceries and cooking implements. But my kitchen also contains various nonfood items such as screwdrivers, cans of spray paint, homework assignments, inner-tube patch kits, overdue library books, at least one yucky sock, a basketball, an orthodontic retainer that's supposed to be worn at all times by the retainee, a terminal philodendron, and a few thousand expired grocery coupons.

To my amazement, Wanda said that by devising a color-coded freezer chart, alphabetizing pantried cans, spices, and packaged products, and tossing out tons of never-used gadgetry, the extra kitchen space would stretch like a ten-month pregnancy.

Immediately, a hundred and six former margarine tubs, dishwasher-warped mugs, and a handful of berry stemmers, melon ballers, basting brushes and jar-lid looseners were dislodged and tossed in the trash—an exercise I found particularly invigorating.

Above the freezer I posted a user-friendly treasure map identifying the exact contents of every aluminum-foiled bundle. Never again would I think I thawed pork chops only to find soggy scraps I had saved for the dog.

Cinnamon behind basil, tomatoes before turnips—within a few hours, shelved foodstuffs were marching like orderly tinned soldiers instead of awry recruits.

I was sagging wearily against the last picture-perfect cabinet's door when the school bus ejected my thundering herd. In an instant, a pizza-seeking football star fumbled through the freezer and wiped out its entire inventory-control chart. Younger Daughter scattered the precisely English pantry into an unintelligible dialect in her quest for crackers, two shelves above. Little Guy salvaged the hundred and six margarine tubs, dishwasher-warped mugs, berry stemmers, melon ballers, basting brushes, and jar-lid looseners for sandbox construction equipment, and I know each piece will eventually find its way back into the drawer or cabinet from whence it came.

At least Wanda Whiteglove was right about something. At the beginning of the article she said she believes that someday, houses will be self-cleaning.

And no doubt, *I'll* still be the "self" cleaning it.

Suburban Renewal

I'm getting the impression that it's time to remodel our home. First, the FBI telephoned, asking to use our hallway as a training area for fingerprint identification specialists.

Then, Older Son complained bitterly of being accosted each morning by the primary-colored "Dinosaurs on Parade" border traipsing around his bathroom—not an unreasonable attitude for one starting his senior year in high school.

But not until Spouse failed to find room for my subcompact automobile within the euphemistically named *two*-car garage did the need for suburban renewal become unanimously apparent.

We knew when we bought a fixit-priced, preloved home that redecorating and renovating was in order. At the time of our purchase, no one shoved rose-colored glasses onto our noses—we alone insisted the hovel's potential for sweat-equitable profits was unlimited.

However, tokens of the former owners' affections were much more obvious after the deed was done than during our preliminary tours. Simply switching fixtured light bulbs from dim watt-nots to daylighting seventy-fives opened our eyes to an abundance of honey-do's and me-too's. Just as we cherish our children—despite their somewhat rough exteriors—the house fairly whimpered for a lot of TLC (Time, Lysol, and Cash), and a minor facelift to smooth its bumps and blemishes.

Unfortunately, various snafus hampered our habitat's reconstructive surgery. Damp and dreary days failed to inspire my Spouse's upward (from the couch) mobility. Warm and sunny weekends clearly illustrated our differing interpretations of the phrase "teed off."

As time Marched, Apriled, and Mayed on, Hubby's imaginative delay tactics ranged from budgetary deficits too severe to finance the necessary materials, to episodes of sciatica soothed by occupying a prone position for seventy-two hours' worth of televised sporting events.

I argued that pressing a plastic card's numbers onto carbon-papered sales receipts relieves those aforementioned economic shortfalls. Or, as the leader of the Light Brigade bellowed at dawn's early light, "Ready . . . Aim . . . C-H-A-R-G-E!"

And I dismissed Spouse's medical malfunctions when it became obvious that only his ability to climb ladders and tote tools was hindered—he certainly didn't seem impaired when he sprinted to the kitchen for snacks during halftime.

While the Women's Liberation Movement effectively freed me to engage in myriad formerly male-monopolized home improvement endeavors, I have neither the skills nor the desire to do so.

My hammering is adequate until nails are involved. Electric drills, saws, sanders, and routers possess more horsepower than I do, but they don't respond to shouted commands to "Whoa!" And I'd be a better painter if I used my head, because that's where most of the paint goes, anyway.

But I was desperate, and so was the house. I began studying our extensive collection of household how-to manuals. After a few hours of plier education, I cheerfully excused my mate from further domestic duties and announced my single-handed intention to scuttle a wall or two, monkey-wrench our plumbing problems, and generally restore our quarters to ship-shapeliness.

(Just as I had hoped, *my* aspirations made Captain Video get *his* in gear.)

In a whiz, fluffy-napped rollers were skimming #117 Pristine Pale Parchment over walls which had formerly been scuffed, scarred, and picture punctured. He who had only known "cut and paste" as computer functions, peeled the bathroom's bouncing brontosauruses and replaced them with a paisley pattern designed for a more mature audience.

Brassy drapery rods gleamed from yonder window frames, and grungy gray ceiling fixtures were scrubbed and restored to crystalline clarity.

The kitchen faucet's floppy stick shift got a new transmission, and ceramic tiles that had stayed in place only by force of habit were expertly regrouted.

For a finale, the Chairman of the Board gathered lumber, tools, and an assortment of adhesive bandages to construct a veritable warehouse of cabinetry in the garage. Now not only can *both* cars rest comfortably under one roof, we no longer need to hide the Dempsey dumpster in the barberry bushes.

Without a doubt, clothes *do* make the man . . . cooperate. In the future, if I have romance in mind, I'll slip on a sexy chemise. But if household maintenance is my heart's desire, I'll buckle on the old tool belt and clank by the couch a few times.

One way or the other, I bet that man'll get a move on, in a hurry.

FOUR

CHILDREN

There's a time when

you have to explain

to your children

why they're born and

it's a marvelous thing

if you know

the reason by then.

—HAZEL SCOTT

Mother Ledbetter's Lunch-box Laws

Because Younger Son seldom eats any food that hasn't danced on television, meal planning can present quite a challenge.

Although my average for making taste-bud tickling dinners is approximately three nights out of seven, he's never needed more than two words to sum up his opinion of his school's cafeteria lunch menus. "Gross" is for Mondays', Wednesdays', and Fridays' fare while "yuck" pretty much covers what's served on Tuesdays and Thursdays.

Since it's been scientifically established that children cannot live—or learn—on bread and butter alone (the only cafeteria-style appetizer Son would dare sink his teeth into), I had no choice but to start packing his lunches at home.

Except assembling a nutritionally balanced meal that won't leak, smell "funny," or turn ptomainic—and that will fit inside a lunch box, and will actually be eaten by the child for whom it was intended—is easier said than done. Especially when the lunch packer must hit that culinarily creative high note at about 7:00 A.M.

Although my years of experience have not turned Son into a galloping gourmet, they have formed the basis of what I call Mother Ledbetter's Lunch-box Laws:

1. Those cute, reusable plastic containers perfect for pudding and applesauce have only a fifty-fifty chance of ever being brought home again. Their lids stand absolutely no chance at all of returning to you.

2. The food editors of parenting magazines who come up with ideas like cutting sandwiches into tummy-tempting cartoon character shapes, and poking whole cloves into peach halves to make smiley faces, should be shot.

3. It is impossible to convince a child that potato chips purchased in large bags for dividing into sandwich bag-sized portions taste exactly the same as those that come in expensive, primarily air-filled baglets manufactured specifically for lunch boxes.

4. Jell-O becomes a beverage by approximately 10:15 A.M.

5. Limiting a child's choices of sandwich fillings to either "smooth" or "crunchy" is a tad unimaginative.

6. It's entirely possible that Robert Oppenheimer got the idea for the atom bomb the day his mother filled his thermos with a carbonated soft drink.

7. If on New Year's evening, you realize your child's lunch box has been in her backpack since the start of Christmas vacation, think of it as toxic waste and dispose of it accordingly.

8. On the same day your child puts his school picture packet in his lunch box for safekeeping, his guaranteed leakproof thermos will rupture.

9. Even if it's your child's favorite meal, wieners and sauerkraut stuffed into an airtight container since sunrise can clear a cafeteria faster than a fire drill.

10. *Never* allow a child to pack her own lunch. While the cheese puffs, frosted cupcakes, baggies full of fruit-ring cereal, and chocolate-covered peanuts you thought were still hidden are filling, this combination will not help her memorize all the states' capitals during afternoon geography class.

11. If the lunch box arrives home completely empty every day, you're either consistently packing yummies your child absolutely *loves*, or consistently packing stuff good enough to trade for other kids' cheese puffs, cupcakes, fruit rings, and chocolate-covered peanuts.

Thankfully, at most, you'll only have to "do lunch" for your child about two thousand, five hundred and twenty times. Once youngsters hit high school, cafeteria fare includes salad and burger bars, pizza parlors, and a gamut of vending-machine munchies.

Then all you'll be packing their lunch boxes with is money.

Parent Speak

Parent Speak is as old as Adam and Eve, a language that's impossible to define, and one which is never taught in a classroom.

The meaning of the words is seldom clear to the children at whom such missives are aimed, but somehow, the message gets across.

Consider these examples from my *Parent Speak Manual of Confusing Commands*:

- ***"Close your mouth and eat your dinner!"***
  This directive is rarely followed by instructions on how the child is supposed to get food into his mouth without opening it, or how he can possibly chew with his jaws in a semi-locked position.
- ***"If you don't stop crying, I'll give you something to cry about!"***
  Typically whispered into a sobbing child's ear and in a public situation. What Parent wants is for Child to turn off the tears so people will stop staring. However, threatening retribution seldom achieves that goal because even a toddler knows that the odds of getting the object of his boohooing desire—gum, candy, quarters for the supermarket horsey—are directly proportional to the number of witnesses frowning their disapproval at Mom.
- ***"Keep your hands where they belong."***
  Scientific studies show that children cannot detach their hands and lay them elsewhere. A matched pair *belongs* at

the end of a child's arms and, unlike mittens, are decidedly difficult to misplace.

- ***"Why don't you act your age?"***
  Have you ever stopped and wondered how a child is supposed to know how to act at any given age, when she has no prior experience at *being* her current chronological age?
- ***"Who do you think you are?"***
  The response to this query is often a goggle-eyed stare, and for good reason. Little Herbert was, until a moment ago, relatively certain he is Little Herbert. Except all of a sudden, his mother thinks he thinks he's someone else.
- ***"How many times have I told you . . ."***
  Might this leave children assuming they'd missed Mother's command to *count*? And responding with top-of-the-head estimates such as "About a million" is rarely appreciated, either.
- ***"I don't want to hear ONE MORE WORD out of you. Do you understand me?"***
  Usually, a two-part ultimatum. If Child obeys by *not* saying another word, Mother immediately contradicts herself by saying: "ANSWER ME!" But a "yes" or "no" reply results in a no-nonsense reminder that not *one more word* was to be heard! For Child, this represents a sometimes-you-just-can't-win situation.
- ***"I know what's best for you" or "I'm your mother, that's why."***
  Meaning: "Because I gained seventy-three pounds, upchucked every morning for two hundred and seventy-nine days, have stretch marks deep enough for a Tonka truck trail, and suffered through seventeen hours of hard labor to *put* you on this planet, I'll spend the rest of my life telling you *exactly* what to do and *exactly* how to do it."

  Can't argue with that one, can you?
- ***"If you fall off of that roof (tree, fence, woodpile, etc.) and break your leg, don't come running to me!"***
  The oxymoronic nature of this statement is apparent to any acrobatically inclined child. After all, how would anyone

run *anywhere* with one's leg broken? Worse yet, if the wee one *did* take a tumble and fracture a fibula, would the parent follow up with: "I warned you, but you wouldn't listen. Now you can just go splint that sucker yourself!"?

If your version of Parent Speak relies more on family tradition than common sense, perhaps it's time to withdraw some confusing commands from your memory bank.

Although using these phrases proves that history, be it world or personal, *does* repeat itself (and probably has since the Garden of Eden), Mother Tongue is hardly a tenet of quality parent/child communications.

In fact, as children grow older, they tend to question the mental stability of any adult who puts an end to splashing in puddles by asking, "Don't you have enough sense to come in out of the rain?" then later sends the same kid out into a monsoonal downpour to fetch the newspaper by saying, "So what if it's raining? You won't melt!"

He Went Which-a-Way?

For years, when vacation travel commences, I've been the Keeper of the Road Map, The Authority on which exit to take, which way we're headed, and what blue highway constitutes a shortcut. Forgive my bragging, but my internal compass is as accurate as a Swiss timepiece.

Unfortunately, Younger Son did not inherit such admirable aim, and his skewed sense of direction is becoming increasingly evident.

For example, Son's bathroom is a convenient three steps forward and one step to the right of his bedroom door. It's been in that location since before he had any real need for most of its fixtures. He has no problem finding this porcelain palace if he wants to wage bubbly sea battles in the tub. He's never needed a map to locate the sink when a muddy plesiosaur needs soaking. But woe is me if he awakens during the night, suddenly seasick.

The bathroom's glowing nightlight notwithstanding, when the urge to pitch his pizza overtakes him, the only two routes Son follows are either a *left* turn into the beige-broadloomed living room, or a straightforward one terminating at my side of the bed. Unless you've experienced a similar situation, you hardly know the meaning of "a rude awakening." But I shouldn't confine my tales of Son's straying to hours after dark.

Even when perfectly healthy and it's daylight, Son is famous for wandering off in odd directions. While his intention may have been to play video games at Mike's house, two doors north of ours, I'll invariably find him shooting baskets in Kevin's driveway, three houses to the *south.*

His explanation for the detour? "I was on the way home from Mike's when Kevin asked me to play Horse."

If I dare ask how Kevin's house, located at least a quarter-mile in the opposite direction of Mike's and reached only by walking directly past and beyond our own, could *possibly* be considered "on his way home," all I get is a shoulder-shrugging "I dunno."

Undoubtedly, if Younger Son had been his navigator, Columbus would have discovered Poland.

Despite directional deviations, this child does have an uncanny ability for tracking hidden treasures. Kind of.

If his only rectangular slant-sided lock block is buried amid 9,741 others, he can excavate the tiny piece of plastic in seconds. But if it lies smack-dab in the middle of the room, he'll be the last one to see it. I'll be the first to step on it.

Or, if I buy a box of marshmallow-middle cupcakes on a school-day afternoon and hide them in the darkest corner of an upstairs crawlspace where none but spiders have gone before, I'll find Son dunking one in his milk before the school bus exits the neighborhood.

But it's a dirty trick for me to hang his jacket in the *closet.* Jeez, he'd never think of looking for it *there.*

This problem seemed insoluble until I decided to play hide-and-seek by Son's rules, rather than insist he follow mine.

Hiding something in plain sight, and/or in his underwear drawer, almost guarantees he won't find it. Tucking things I want him to find into closet corners assures he *will.* And when seeking Son, I now check the least likely location *first*; more often than not, he's there.

Not only has this technique decreased my nag reflex and made mothering a misguided male a more pleasant experience, my son's respect for me has risen appreciably.

Mostly because he just can't figure out how I got so smart all of a sudden.

The Unstrung Quartet

Resting on our fireplace mantel are four tiny pairs of bronzed baby booties, all with the shoelaces untied. By permanently preserving these mementos of my children's toddlerhoods, I had no idea I was forecasting their footwearing future.

It was not until I had four offspring of my own that I understood why my mother had always encouraged *me* to skip about barefooted. I thought she was saving shoe leather. Actually, she was saving her sanity.

First, it seems that none of my children can remove both shoes within the same geographical area. If a right shoe's in the living room, the left may lie in the bathtub, the basement, or abandoned next door at Billy's house.

Although I was taught to untie my shoes before removing them, this concept has not caught on with my kids. Instead, they simply force their feet *out* of their tightly laced tennies. Because shoestrings don't appreciate being stretched in this fashion, they retaliate by either gnarling themselves into enormous knots like no sailor has ever seen, or inconveniently snapping in half.

Therefore, putting small bodies and soles together for an outing is a frustrating experience for all concerned. The presence of four children means the absence of at least two pairs of matching shoes. Searching under beds and in toy boxes for suitable mates takes time, and is often accompanied by my observation that said youngsters' heads and hindquarters might also be misplaced if not permanently attached.

Once the number of shoes available equals the number of

feet in need, a fork must be implemented to dislodge the aforementioned knots. This chore requires incredible patience, manual dexterity, and numerous adhesive bandages to hide my self-inflicted stab wounds. Replacing the entire lace is usually out of the question since extra shoestrings go the route of all those other never-to-be-found-when-you-need-them objects.

Because children tend to declare their independence at the worst possible times, pleas to "Let me tie your shoes for you, just this once" are met with stubborn refusal. If at first she doesn't succeed, it'll be try, try, *try* again until perfect double loopers are done. No matter how l-o-n-g it takes.

Due to this footwear futility, I seldom treat my tribe to restaurant meals because an inside-seatable establishment usually has a "No Shoes, No Service" policy. And as any mother knows, carpooling kids farther than a hundred yards from home means at least one of them becomes shoeless again before the destination is reached.

Either the entire unknotting/retying process must then be repeated (during which a sibling is likely to lose his shoe, too) or the choice of restaurant must be reconsidered.

Those who think drive-through service was invented for time-crunched adults are mistaken. Only parents of several starving, semishod children are desperate enough to shout menu selections into a plastic whale's waterspout.

Self-closing fasteners on sneakers have been promoted as a cure for the loose-shoe blues, and they do stay stuck temporarily. But grass clippings, lint, dog hair, and one thread guaranteed to unravel the wearer's entire sock will inevitably gum up the works.

Eventually, my children's shoe-tying speed *increased*, but proportionately, their desire to do so *decreased*. Day after day they loped along trailing shoestrings long enough to rig a small sailboat.

Since reminding them to tie their shoes was about as effective as reminding them to flush, I asked why they refused to use the shoe skills I had so lovingly and left-handedly taught them.

Their answer was twofold: (1) Tying wasted at least three seconds of their precious eighteen-hour playtime. (2) More important, according to teenaged trendsetters starring in their favorite television sitcoms, only NERDS wore tied shoes. From the looks of their laces, none of my children *ever* need fear being labeled with the N-word.

Between leading sneaker search parties, unknotting, retying, and (within seconds) watching all my efforts come unstrung again, I've decided that if reincarnation is possible, I want to spend my next life as a horse: *Its* children's shoes are *nailed* to their feet. With no strings attached.

The Twelve Weeks of Summer

On the first week of summer, my four kids gave to me
A pledge to be good, you will see.

On the second week of summer, my four kids gave to me
Two migraine headaches
And a pledge to be good, you will see.

On the third week of summer, my four kids gave to me
Three scrapes a-bleeding,
Two migraine headaches,
And a pledge to be good, you will see.

On the fourth week of summer, my four kids gave to me
Four tons of laundry,
Three scrapes a-bleeding,
Two migraine headaches,
And a pledge to be good, you will see.

On the fifth week of summer, my four kids gave to me
Five trips a-malling,
Four tons of laundry,
Three scrapes a-bleeding,
Two migraine headaches,
And a pledge to be good, you will see.

On the sixth week of summer, my four kids gave to me
Six friends a-playing,

Five trips a-malling,
Four tons of laundry,
Three scrapes a-bleeding,
Two migraine headaches,
And a pledge to be good, you will see.

On the seventh week of summer,
my four kids gave to me
Seven swains arriving,
Six friends a-playing,
Five trips a-malling,
Four tons of laundry,
Three scrapes a-bleeding,
Two migraine headaches,
And a pledge to be good, you will see.

On the eighth week of summer, my four kids gave to me
Eight daily fridge raids,
Seven swains arriving,
Six friends a-playing,
Five trips a-malling,
Four tons of laundry,
Three scrapes a-bleeding,
Two migraine headaches,
And a pledge to be good, you will see.

On the ninth week of summer, my four kids gave to me
Nine playmates arguing,
Eight daily fridge raids,
Seven swains arriving,
Six friends a-playing,
Five trips a-malling,
Four tons of laundry,
Three scrapes a-bleeding,
Two migraine headaches,
And a pledge to be good, you will see.

On the tenth week of summer, my four kids gave to me
Ten cries of boredom,
Nine playmates arguing,
Eight daily fridge raids,
Seven swains arriving,
Six friends a-playing,
Five trips a-malling,
Four tons of laundry,
Three scrapes a-bleeding,
Two migraine headaches,
And a pledge to be good, you will see.

On the eleventh week of summer, my four kids gave to me
Eleven gripes and grumbles,
Ten cries of boredom,
Nine playmates arguing,
Eight daily fridge raids,
Seven swains arriving,
Six friends a-playing,
Five trips a-malling,
Four tons of laundry,
Three scrapes a-bleeding,
Two migraine headaches,
And a pledge to be good, you will see.

On the twelfth week of summer, my four kids gave to me
Twelve sports a-practicing,
Eleven gripes and grumbles,
Ten cries of boredom,
Nine playmates arguing,
Eight daily fridge raids,
Seven swains arriving,
Six friends a-playing,
Five trips a-malling,
Four tons of laundry,
Three scrapes a-bleeding,
Two migraine headaches,
And a pledge to be good, you will see.

ON THE THIRTEENTH WEEK OF SUMMER,
THE SCHOOL BOARD GAVE TO ME:

Mandatory attendance,
Seven hours of quiet,
Closed campus lunching,
Bus transport daily,

And I pledge to be good, you will see.

School Daze

It's easy for a mother to identify the beginning of another school year when she sees the school bus pause along its route and load her children. But here are other, more subtle signs that the books-and-backpack season has begun:

• The telephone rings and the caller asks for *me*. Though the person on the incoming end may only want to sell me steel siding or a magazine subscription, or solicit a contribution to a charitable organization, it's nice to know my presence in the home is still noticeable and that my telephone responses aren't limited to "I'll get him," "No, she's not home right now," and "Oh, no, not again! I'll be there as soon as I call a tow truck."

• After I load the dishwasher with postbreakfast bowls, spoons, juice glasses, and plates, I can rest assured that the kitchen sink will remain empty for several hours.

• If anyone's voices are amplified by the television's speakers, it's Phil's or Oprah's, not Mr. Rogers's, Kermit the Frog's, or any heavy-metal rock band's lead singer's.

• Grocery-store runs and jaunts to the discount store, the post office, the bank, dry cleaner's, and hardware emporium are accomplished in half the time required during the months of June through August. Plus, such errands no longer necessitate stops for fast food snacks, or set off I-wanna-/will-you-buy-me-/how-come-I-can't-have-/I'll-pay-you-back-later tug-of-roar debates.

• I can close the bathroom door without the fear of hinge-rattling fists whomping on it within milliseconds, or the bellowing of tactless inquiries such as: "Hey, Mom! Whatcha doin' in there?" originating from the other side.

• Dusted furniture, vacuumed carpeting, waxed floors, made beds, clean dishes, and folded laundry stay that way until the school bus returns.

• I get first dibs on the daily newspaper, subscription magazines, and the mail, and sole proprietorship of the radio channel selector knob and the television's remote control gizmo for several hours each day.

• There will be no tattletale reports of my purchasing a new outfit or having lunch in a restaurant. Afternoons spent languishing behind a steamy romance novel or napping on the sofa stay my little secrets.

• At least six hours' daily respite from auditory assaults such as: "Can I . . . ?," "Will you . . . ?," "He hit . . . ," "She took . . . ," "Make him stop . . . ," "I'm gonna tell . . . ," "Why can't I . . . ," and the oft-bellowed "M-O-M-M-M-M-M-!"

• My husband has suddenly begun coming home for lunch, but a grilled cheese sandwich and potato chips isn't always the menu he has in mind.

• I can discard the names of available daytime baby-sitters and Mother's Day Out program schedules from their summertime places of honor on the refrigerator door.

• No one will be certain whether I personally hand-assembled an apple pie for dessert or bought the frozen brand best befitting the circumference of my own pie tin; or whether I really damp-mopped the whole kitchen floor or just grabbed a wet paper towel and scrubbed the yucky spots. And no one—ever—will know I rewarded myself with a teensy-weensy ice-cream cone after being such a calorie-conscious good girl all day.

With all these joyous moments of solitary seclusion after serving a one-hundred-day sentence of what only children could term summer "vacation," I'm always surprised to find that the peace and quiet I'd yearned for seems a tad too peaceful and spookily quiet.

It's strange how those lists of itemized "want-to-dos" I penned and promised myself when the kids were again within the halls of higher learning no longer seem as important or exciting as they did when I jotted them down.

And who would have believed I'd be standing in the window watching for the bus to come back with the same foot-tapping impatience with which I awaited its morning arrival?

Cashless Society

I can't understand why financial forecasters are so excited about the concept of a "cashless society." As a mother of four, I've been cashless for years but I don't see any reason to brag about it.

Hard as I've tried to keep my bucks in a row and preferably in my billfold, my children can smell the ink on freshly minted money from miles away. And each of them mastered the economic principle of "supply and demand" at approximately the age of prekindergarten screening. As soon as my quartet of children smells the scent of stashed cash, demands for dollars for lunch, gasoline, tickets for a school activity, a date, a dress, or the latest tress-management mousse, guaranteed to stand their hair fashionably on end, spew forth.

If a funding request is a mere two dollars and all I have is a ten-dollar bill, I know the excess eight dollars will not be seen or heard of again. To my offspring, *change* is like *homework*: No matter how often I ask if they have any, the answer is always "No."

Hoping to cure my constant cashlessness, I bought a how-to manual chock-full of ideas for teaching children how to manage money. Although my children were already adept at managing *mine*, the booklet's author offered twenty-six alphabetized tips on teaching minor bank account robbers better budgeting systems.

Plan A advised each child to carefully calculate the amount needed per week for expenses and list the chores they would do regularly to earn it. This supposedly planted the idea that even if money grew on trees, someone had to fertilize the forest occasionally.

Alas, my children's domestic duty roster included such Trojanlike toils as petting the dog, choosing which brands of supermarketed cookies, cereal, and soda pop to buy, and "helping Mommy tape movies with the VCR." The fee for all this live-in household help was only two hundred dollars per week. Each.

Plan B recommended graphing my *own* task table with a payment schedule for each completed job. For example, one dollar could be earned for trundling the trash, three dollars for a whole-house vacuuming, five for a car wash-and-wax, or fifty cents for setting the dinner table. Not only would this allow freedom of choice, willing workers could finance loans to the lazy—with interest rates compounded hourly.

The pay-as-you-go plan enjoyed temporary success, but eventually the children wanted a gratuity for *everything*: If dusting was worth a dollar, wasn't flushing worth a dime? Dishwashing paid seventy-five cents, so showering should net a quarter, right? And in either case, soap was extra.

Before they began billing me for breathing, I declared reorganizational bankruptcy.

Because plans C through Z were comparably profound philosophies, it became apparent that this authoritative author was either independently wealthy, or childless.

Regardless of what the future promises, increasing my children's sense of fiscal responsibility has a definite link to our country's history. Like the battles fought by General George Armstrong Custer, sometimes I'll win; sometimes I'll lose; and sometimes I'll just get scalped.

High Praise, Indeed

If I've told my children once that they look pretty/handsome/nice/kind-of-clean, I've told them a thousand times.

And on days when "My, you're growing! Your handprints are so much higher on the wall than they used to be!" is as much flattery as I can muster, I do try heaping on the praise whenever possible.

Problem is, while my muttering of a naughty noun will undoubtedly be repeated and its source cited during Sunday school, offerings of kindlier words are seldom recycled in a "The more you give, the more you will receive" manner.

For example, if I stride spiffily by the breakfast table wearing the first new outfit purchased since the Reagans departed the White House, do I hear, "Gee, Mommy, you sure look pretty!"?

Maybe, but more likely I'll hear, "Hey! Is that a new outfit? No *wonder* you said you couldn't afford that Hyper-Turbo X-47A Supersonic Hovercraft I wanted."

For this I've spent half my life cutting brownies into precisely centimetered squares? Ridden the Tilt-A-Whirl two hundred and seventy-three times? Frozen my muffs off waiting for the float carrying my exceptionally grim-looking little elves to pass by during a Christmas parade?

If Younger Son uses the snow shovel as a room cleaning tool, I'm supposed to applaud his ingenuity and hustle, despite the fact that I know, lurking behind those closed closet doors, is an avalanche just waiting to happen.

But if *I* spend the whole day scrubbing away a houseful of dust, accumulated dreck, and megamesses not of my making, *my* efforts are rewarded with at least one of the following responses:

- "Are we having company?"
- "Gosh, I didn't know you'd put the house up for sale!"
- "Hey! Where'd you hide my STUFF?"
- "What'cha been doin' all day, Mom?"

Or, let's say I've resisted the urge to dial for a delivered pizza *again*, and have instead put a sirloin on the grill, rolled some #1 Idaho bakers into the oven, speckled a salad with croutons and real-bacon bacon bits, and set the table not only with place mats, but have a bowl of mashy-sweet strawberries piled high as a centerpiece. What will I hear when these culinary love tokens are sighted?

"Steak? *And* strawberry shortcake? Wow! Who's coming over for dinner?"

While all such remarks presume that a preguest frenzy is the only time I detox the domestic environment, and that family-only fare is limited to gruel and tap water, that scenario is simply not true.

By Heloise, I work my fingers to veritable *bones* during national holidays and months with blue moons too, but what I *do* do rarely receives the attention that what I *don't* get done does.

Eventually, a collective of noncredit comments causes the bursting forth of a speech I call "Ask *Not* What Your Mother Can Do for You; Ask What *You* Can Do for Your Mother" that invariably falls upon, goes in, and directly out of, four pairs of selectively deaf ears.

Since the kitchen faucet has proven a more captive and sympathetic audience for my tales of woe, next thing I know, I'm up to my elbows in bubbles, toiling and troubling over what a fine set of ungrateful, selfish, lazy louts I've foaled, and I'll feel a tug on my shirttail and hear a soft voice warble, "Turn around. I gots a surprise for you."

And there will be a heel-rocking, muddy-cheeked cherub, clutching a fistful of root-dangly, wilty dandelions.

"I love you, Mommy," the little angel lisps, stretching to give me the world's loveliest bouquet.

And once again I'm reminded: There are no words my children can ever say that will mean more to me than those.

Yep, that's high praise, *indeed.*

How Much Is That Burfer in the Window?

The American Kennel Club recognizes a hundred and twenty-nine pure breeds of dogs as eligible for membership in their organization. These estimable blue bloods are subdivided into descriptive groupings such as: working, hunting, small, large, and rare.

But when children start begging for a pet, I use a much simpler rating system in which breeding, or the lack thereof, matters little. Instead of all this folderol of traced bloodlines, I'd rather pick a pooch by discerning whether it's a Yipper, Whoofer, or Burfer.

My doggie categories pertain more to the personality and the way the animal barks than whether or not its ancestors were as sterling as those of Great Britain's Royal Family. For those who are more concerned with living happily ever after with a four-legged friend than with knowing its ancestry, here is the trio of traits that makes up my method of choosing canine companions.

A *Yipper* is the soprano section of the dog world. Its bark has the same effect on human ears as "skrees" emitted when fingernails scrape a blackboard. These dogs frequently alert their owners and surrounding neighbors to emergencies such as leaves falling from trees, a change in the wind direction, the location of the moon, and the arrival of the mail, a garbage truck, the meter reader, the newspaper carrier, and every other residential coming and going within a two-block radius.

Unfortunately, if a Yipper's home is invaded by burglars,

it'll hide mutely under a bed until the danger has passed. A Yipper is a true watchdog; it'll watch silently as thieves abscond with your property.

In addition, most Yippers are small dogs with inbred Napoleon complexes. They tend to exhibit this psychological quirk by nipping a friendly visitor's ankle with their teensy, razor-sharp incisors for no apparent reason other than a wave of insecurity suddenly striking the Yipper's damaged psyche. For that reason alone, I'd remain dogless before I'd tuck a Yipper-snapper under my arm and carry it home.

Whoofers are the exact opposites of Yippers. Their physical size exceeds that of my car, they tend to be long-haired, shed copiously, and though by virtue of size may *look* ferocious, Whoofers would only endanger the boogeyman if he stood still long enough to be licked to death.

The only people Whoofers actually do frighten are family members—particularly Mom. Whoofers take great pride in sneaking up behind her and unleashing a loud "whoof!" at Mom's unsuspecting back. How high she rises from the floor, her hang time, and the spiciness of her language upon landing is invariably answered with wheezy doggie laughter. Whoofers do love attention, and this is one sure-fire way to get it.

A Whoofer may be lovable, but he'll eat chow by the ton and drink water by the gallon. He'll spend most of his time napping in doorways or sprawled on a bed, but Whoofers do know quality, and will only snooze on custom-made, dry-clean-only, pastel-colored comforters.

I've avoided owning a dog in this canine category not only for the reasons stated above, but because most Whoofers are too large to fit into my car for the annual veterinary checkup. The combination of a subcompact automobile and a full-sized dog creates a situation where Whoofer has nowhere to hang his weary head (and constantly salivating tongue) other than over the front seat and above my right shoulder. Though some consider Whoofers the kings of the dog world, I'd rather they rained over someone else.

In my experienced estimation, the best dog to have is a *Burfer.* Burfers don't ambush, nip, Whoof or Yip; they simply "burf"—a form of communication easiest for humans to understand.

Depending on what he wants to convey, Burfer may use a low-throated, soft "burf" to ask for a nice head rub, or a higher-pitched "*burrff*" accompanied by a grin when he's ready to play. A series of "Burf-Burf-BURFBURFBURF's" will promptly alert a master to danger.

Burfers come in all sizes, but medium-sized is usually best for a family. Big enough to be easily seen and not tripped over, but small enough to curl quietly in a sun-warmed corner, mid-sized Burfers are loved by children because they are tireless and patient outdoor playmates and furry, warm, cartoon-time cuddlers.

The first Burfer I adopted was a puppy, ostensibly chosen for the children. Advertised as a German shepherd/Irish setter mix, he definitely had his daddy's floppy ears and his mommy's pointed nose, even if the sum of his other parts could have touched off an International Incident.

In honor of his December birth, and because his glossy coat was rather reddish, I named him Saint Nicholas—shortened almost immediately to "Nick." (We soon learned that although he was clumsily adorable, he was no saint.)

Spouse's attitude regarding the pup was simple: He would never feed it, bathe it, or walk it, and he'd better never go into the kitchen in the middle of the night and step in it.

Nick knew instinctively that Spouse was not his best friend, so, in typically dumb dog fashion, proceeded to haunt his master's every move. This prompted my husband to frequently refer to the dog by using a descriptive noun that only rhymed with "Nick."

One of the games the pup loved to play with Spouse was a version of Keep Away. Whenever hubby was outdoors in fix-it mode and laid down a tool, Nick delightedly pounced on it, then ran back a few yards. As hubby approached to reclaim his property, the dog deftly retreated again. This artful dodging continued until my husband gave up and stomped into the house muttering words rhyming with "it."

Not all Burfers are as mischievous as Nick (nor are all husbands as poetic), but when it comes to finding a pet to steal the hearts and hammers of every member of your family, take my advice and buy a Burfer.

Mama and the Four-speed Locker Room

When I became a licensed driver, I thought parental presentation of a perky little sports car was an inalienable right, as granted by the U.S. Constitution. What I *got* was the right to borrow my dad's clunky '57 Chevy. To my horrified eyes, that seafoam-green, rust-scabbed monster's only Constitutional correlation was to the *ship* named for it.

Lack of funds precluded owning a sports car during my single days, and marriage and the arrival of four children demanded no less than an enormous, wood-sided, luggage-racked station wagon. Although handy for hauling everything from progeny and playmates to plywood and peat moss, this vehicle held no relationship to a sports car either—other than being big enough to have birthed one.

Thankfully, my need for a multiseated vehicle waned at about the same time Daughter passed *her* driver's test and gained part-time, after-school employment. Her ambitious spirit was undoubtedly born of the belief that by earning *her* own spending money, Spouse and I would be delighted to spend *ours* on a set of get-to-work wheels.

All of a sudden, what my parents had meant by "You'll understand when you have children of your own" was abundantly clear: Sane adults do not buy shiny new cars for shiny new drivers. Besides, as Spouse and I had frequently been called the least understanding, most strict, most unfair pair of parents on the planet, we didn't want to ruin our image.

Due to the station wagon's numerous dents and dings,

dangling chrome trim, and a passenger door that only a swift kick to the side panel could open, it had long been nicknamed The Beast. Granting Daughter, an unquestionable Beauty, our permission to drive it seemed quite appropriate.

The moment Beauty and The Beast groaned off into the sunset together, I dashed to the nearest car dealership to finally fulfill my dreams of a snazzy maroon subcompact with a smooth-as-a-baby's-bottom exterior, houndstooth-checkered interior, and all the options *I* considered mandatory in a sports car, including:

- Manual transmission, reminiscent of my learn-to-drive days. (Since Daughter hadn't a clue how to clutch and no desire to learn, there was no way she could borrow it, either.)
- An AM-*only* radio, because all area rock-music stations broadcast on FM airwaves.
- Last but not least, a four-seat maximum seating capacity to end my transportation of every kid in the neighborhood to any and all school-sponsored events (a plus only veteran carpoolers can fully appreciate).

Unfortunately, I'd only owned my dream machine a few days when I learned the term "*sports* car" has a second definition: a four-speed, mobile locker room. Because of two actively athletic sons, my car quickly took on all the ambience and aroma of their shoulder pads, helmets, cleated footwear, and drippy sweat suits, which dispel any doubt as to what boys do while wearing them.

And what but a *sports* car develops a starboard tilt due to linebacker-sized passengers?

Only a true *sports* car's upholstery is dabbled with the chilidog droppings, ketchup glops, and chocolate-syrup smears resulting from numerous pre- and post-practice fast feedings.

OK, so my wheels are still shy of gee-whizzy, but whenever I drive it, at least I flaunt the same wind-mussed and wanton look *real* sports car drivers do.

After all, with the cargo I'm carrying, you think I can go anywhere with the windows rolled *up*?

Parental Invisibility

Once upon a time, you probably had American Express–style relationships with your children: You seldom left home without them. Then with adolescence came a role reversal, and your children wanted to get as far away from *you* as possible.

Because knowing when to shine and when to stay in the shadows is mandatory for parents whose teenage children are in this pain-in-the-butt stage, consider the following green-light activities:

• *Shopping:* If your son's or daughter's friends see you occupying the same 13,462,841-square-foot mall, it will be assumed you're "spying" regardless of whether the next closest K-Mart is forty-three miles away.

To avoid such misunderstandings, plant yourself on a bench in a centralized location. When Teen has found and put on hold several zillion dollars' worth of clothes, scattered amid several stores, retrace his/her steps, plunk down your charge card until the plastic softens from overuse, lug all the stuff to the car because your kids have already vanished, and go home where you belong.

They'll remember your generosity someday and thank you, scant seconds before you sign over power of attorney to your estate.

• *Doctor and dental appointments:* If for no other reason than because they're minors, you're needed on these outings for parental consent and for filling out insurance forms. However, unless invited otherwise, stay in the waiting area, please. You wouldn't want your teen in the examination room with *you*, would you?

• *Church:* Teens may *ride* with their parents, but will *sit* elsewhere during the service. Singing hymns and simultaneously neck-craning to ascertain their whereabouts is not only tacky, it reveals a decided lack of faith in a higher power—yours *and* His.

• *Family functions (weddings, reunions, and vacations):* While it's unlikely that reproachful peers will see your teen during family functions, they're still in the realm of the decidedly uncool, so if Teen refuses attendance by exhibiting a stubbornness you hadn't seen since the Terrible Twos, compromise and allow her to ask a friend along. Misery *does* love company.

• *School activities:* It's been said that parents who take time and are interested in teens' extracurricular activities are appreciated greatly for their support. Except, like during church services, there's not much use saving the kid a bleacher seat, or expecting much beyond a nonchalant "Hi," muttered in that heartfelt "Gee, don't I know you from somewhere?" tone.

Having mastered the green-light list, you're ready to learn the *verboten*:

• *Movies:* Since most kids over twelve absolutely do *not* go to movies with their parents, the "Under seventeen must be accompanied by parent or guardian" rating is patently absurd.

• *School dances and parties:* Like acne, parental chauffeuring is a teenage rite of passage, but the designated driver shall not, under any circumstances, exit the automobile, honk the horn, or shout, "Don't do anything I wouldn't, heh-heh-heh," or, "Yoo hoo! Here I am!" out the open window.

As for the chaperoning of school dances, leave that to the geeks' parents. That's why their kids are geeks.

• *School cafeteria/classroom:* Never "catch" your teen during lunch hour to deliver a message, money, or a forgotten textbook or musical instrument. You'll be as recognizable as last week's mystery meat and just about as welcome.

• *The workplace:* Young children delight in visiting a parent's office, but for teens, it's often an embarrassment. While long-time co-workers will coo, "My, what a pretty young lady/handsome young man you're becoming!" the newer staffers will stare as if the kid were part-Klingon.

In spite of the caveats above, you can prevent yourself and your teens from becoming ships passing in the night. Try these remedies for the tiresome teenage years:

• *Rent movies* for home-showing and let Teen choose the title(s). Granted, *Brain-sucking Aliens from the Planet Gore* probably isn't your idea of entertainment, but remember, much of parenting does involve sacrifice.

• *Cook together:* Weight-conscious adolescents like experimenting with new, lo-cal recipes, and Always Hungrys should learn their way around the kitchen to stave off potential starvation. And obviously, at this age, if they're spending time in the kitchen, they're not *making* time, elsewhere. (Heh-heh-heh.)

• *Work together:* Saying, "I really need your help . . ." can clear an area of all young, able-bodied assistants faster than a misfired SCUD missile. But those who don't hear your plea due to heavy-metal "music" pounding in their headphones are fair game. Plan your strategies accordingly.

• *Have an Open House Policy:* Make your teens' friends feel welcome even if your home's decibel level, telephone tie-ups, increasingly lived-in appearance, and grocery budget are swelling like a cobra with an attitude.

I promise that stocking colas and snacks, and cheerfully stretching four pork chops to feed six, won't turn your hair gray; not knowing where your teen is, whom he's with, and what he's doing, *will.*

Spouse and I never gave any of this tiresome teenage stuff a preconceived moment's thought. Neither will our kids when they're grown and begatting the next generation. That's the payback for all these trials and tribulations, the real reason so many older adults want grandchildren so-o-o-o badly: revenge!

Warning: Adolescence Approaching

Parents discover that a baby sits unaided at about six months of age, becomes a cuddly charmer at age three, a student by six, and at ten, a fascinating conversationalist. But when does adolescence begin? As with all stages of child development, the onset of teendom will vary, but the following should serve as a guideline:

• Once upon a time, you had to drag your child from every discount store's Toy Department. Suddenly, the Automotive or Beauty Aids section has the same mesmerizing effect.

• According to the yard-long sales receipt at the supermarket and the total at the bottom which rivals the national debt, Mr. Picky is now consuming everything remotely resembling food, and must be *drinking* the damned shampoo.

• The same child who only occupied her bedroom when sent there for disciplinary reasons, or sleep, is now seldom seen leaving it. And the door is *always* shut. And you can't hear a *thing* through it.

• Was it only yesterday that she thought a twenty-five-cent tooth-fairy tribute was a veritable windfall? Today, a ten-dollar weekly allowance is considered serf's wages and hardly worth the effort it takes to hold out her hand.

• Dinner-table speeches lambasting the parents' generation for carelessly wasting America's precious natural resources are followed by Captain Conservation's sixth hot shower of the day.

• She who was famous for excavating mud-crusted ensembles from the clothes hamper has started shedding from the skin out at least four times daily. And since those clean, ironed, perfectly pristine garments worn for no more than forty-five seconds are now deemed "dirty," they're crammed into the aforementioned clothes hamper, or tossed onto the floor.

• Imparting parental wisdom once received hugs. Now it's shrugs, accompanied by heaven-turned eyes and melancholy sighs.

• The amount expended monthly on acne preventatives, acne treatments, and acne camouflage is roughly equal to the rent you and spouse paid for your post-honeymoon apartment.

• She who says your roast beef, baked potato and green salad supper is chocked with cholesterol goes out with friends for super-deluxe, extra-cheese pizzas.

• Any home lacking cabled MTV, two telephone lines, and an equalized, digitized stereo system with freezer-sized speakers *might* as well be in *Moscow*, for God's sake.

• He who never missed 6:30 A.M. Saturday cartoons now rarely bails out of bed before noon.

Watching a child's metamorphosis into adulthood is no less fascinating, rewarding, and awe-inspiring than witnessing a butterfly's struggle from its cocoon.

Of course in humans, this process takes a lot longer, and living with a freedom-frantic, highly emotional adolescent is like tap-dancing in a minefield: You'll never know when an explosion will occur.

Adolescence is not as much a chronological age as an attitudinal one. Those in the grip of growing uppitiness are absolutely positive they know all the answers. When a teen becomes equally sure he hasn't thought of most of the questions yet, maturity is on the brink.

Gee, and you thought toilet training was tough.

Goin' to the Chapel and We're Gonna Get Married

What can a mother do when Daughter decides June will not only be the month of her high school graduation but also her *wedding*?

Insisting my Juliet was too young, absolutely must continue her education and/or seek gainful employment, and simply not ready for postmatrimonial responsibility was a complete waste of carbon dioxide. She and her Romeo were determined to tie the knot.

During the preceding decade, I'd questioned a kazillion of her actions and attitudes by snipping, "Oh, why don't you grow *up*." Except now that she *has*, she's *also* certain she's the most insightful, intelligent representative of our species. And to prove it, she announced her betrothal, which caused me to automatically wail, "But you're just a *baby*!"

Obviously, deciding whether or not you believe your child capable of surviving adulthood's slings and arrows and ordering a Big Mac with or without sauce are similar: You absolutely cannot have it *both ways*.

Dancing with delight isn't the proper response either because children know instinctively when a parent is performing solely for their benefit—i.e., the Santa Claus/Easter Bunny/Tooth Fairy syndrome.

However, since I gained a wealth of hindsighted "smarts" while waging the Wedding Wars, I feel it only fair to pass this knowledge on to my loyal readers, along with my sincerest wishes that you'll never have reason to use it.

First, a prospective and terrified mother-of-the-bride should purchase current issues of every magazine pertinent to traditional wedding planning. They're easy to spot on the newsstand because they're as hefty as a major metropolitan telephone directory.

Although your Juliet says she dreams of a sunrise service in a wildflowered meadow, let her leaf through scads of photos featuring Chantilly lace, candle-lit cathedrals, and tuxedoed and taffetaed attendants rivaling those in a royal rite. This is *guaranteed* to inspire the immediate envisioning of a fabulously formal ceremony complete with horse-drawn carriages and crated champagne—and a hefty tab, too—BUT! It matters not whether your billfold, bank account, or credit-card ceiling can underwrite the expense of such a wondrous wedding. The key to this strategy is *time.*

It is virtually impossible to arrange such an extravaganza in less than one *year.* Since the expertise of florists, caterers, photographers, musicians, tuxedo tailors, and seamstresses, plus chapel space and a reception room, must all be reserved well in advance, there can be no hasty-to-the-altar affair.

Therefore, setting Juliet's heart on a majestic marriage ceremony, the date of which to be at least fifty-two weeks hence, allows a grace period long enough for either partner's heels to cool.

OK, so there's a teensy chance that her original, pastureized plan will be reinstated, but after memorizing the aforementioned matrimony manuals, nine out of ten female fiancées prefer wedding a morning-suited Prince Charming to a Union-suited mere prince. If they didn't, bridal magazines could be published as *Cliffs Notes.*

If all this sounds contrary to the parenting skills taught by talk-show experts (who shall remain childless), calm your qualms by remembering: This is your daughter's *future* you're so lovingly manipulating.

For her own good, didn't you take her to Sunday school, help her with homework, slather Mercurochrome on scraped knees, and teach her to cross streets safely, never pet strange dogs, or take candy from strangers? Well, this is no time to *stop* those paranoid protection policies—it's just the approach that needs a new spin.

Postpubescent people must be handled with a great deal more subtlety than in the past, when you were believed at least minimally intelligent. Youth, vitality, and vows of undying affection are a potent combination, but the necessity of selecting every "nitpickin' damned detail" from announcements to zinnias can cause even the most devoted duos to see a side of their prospective mate's personality they never had before.

If you recall, despite a veritable army of assistants and a sky's-the-limit budget, even Diana Spencer's tiara got tilted a few times before Prince Charles made a "Lady" of her.

Don't be surprised when Romeo's disinterest in whether rosebuds or gladiolas should spray the chancel is perceived as thoughtlessness. And your Juliet's attention to cummerbund coordination will be called obsessive/compulsive. Factor in his choice of best man (who undoubtedly tops her list of worst enemies) or her dream of a honeymoon cruise as opposed to his idea for a camping trip, and soon lovely Juliet will be shrieking, "ARE YOU OUT OF YOUR @#$%&* *MIND*?"

One word of caution: If familiarity does *not* breed contempt, if your well-meant interference fails to bring the desired result, and if the sumptuous show *must* go on, the fact that you are not losing a daughter but gaining a son *must* be gracefully accepted (or at least faked, admirably).

With careful budgeting, this *what-love-has-joined-together* occasion shouldn't cost much more than that brand-new, three-bedroom, two-bath rancher you and your hubby bought back in 'sixty-four. And with luck, the bills for Juliet's wedding extravaganza will be paid off before the *divorce-do-they-part* part is final.

Now honestly, from the first moment you laid eyes on that pink-pillowed bundle of sugar and spice and everything nice, didn't you promise to give her all the best things Life had to offer? Then, like it or not, the time has come to put your money where your mouth was.

Just as I have.

Twice.

So far.

Ono

At this stage of life, I carry as many identifying labels as a well-traveled steamer trunk: daughter, sister, wife, mother, and aunt.

As if I needed another—and without allowing me an opportunity to state my preconceived notions on the subject—thanks to my daughter and son-in-law, I'll soon get a new one: *grandmother.*

The concept of becoming someone's grandmother on approximately the same date one son celebrates his seventeenth birthday, and another's fifth-grade science class tours the local sewage treatment facility, is mind-boggling.

Is it really so selfish to admit, when my nest has only half-emptied and I have not yet attended my twenty-fifth high school reunion, that:

- I'm not ready to cast aside page-turning novels packed with romance and intrigue to read *Goodnight, Moon* aloud another one thousand, three hundred and forty-seven times?
- If anyone gets an afternoon nap, it ought to be me?
- The only bottles my refrigerator has become accustomed to cooling contain steak sauce, catsup, and fruity wine coolers?
- I pat my children on the back after each hard-earned accomplishment, but am glad they can all burp *themselves*?
- I break out in a red, itchy rash just thinking about changing diapers again?
- I can't visualize my mud-splattered, spike-haired eleven-

year-old who wears his T-shirts backward, still gets Tooth Fairy tributes, and hasn't entirely written off the possibility of Santa Claus, as anybody's uncle?

In all honesty, the realities of *mothering* four of America's Hopes for the Future occasionally send shock waves through my system. And I'm just beginning to learn what *my* mother meant when she said, "You'll understand when you have children of your own."

It was a threat.

Lord only knows what grandmotherdom will do to me. I assumed it wouldn't occur until after the turn of the century. By then, I thought:

- All my furniture would match and I'd care enough to dust my very best—and often.
- I'd be rinsing my hair with Pale Palomino or Elegant Ebony even though my natural shade is more akin to Tree Bark.
- "Dinner for two" would refer to every evening's meal, not just a restaurant reservation.
- Menopause would be the distant memory of a hormonal uprising, not a feature of my future.
- More than seven years would pass between selling my youngest child's car seat at a garage sale and buying another to safely secure the next generation.
- Spouse and I would be *retiring* from full-time employment, not still *tiring* from full-time employment.

I've even had trouble concocting a properly grandmotherish alias. Granted, it will be at least a year before this imminent infant can be expected to communicate verbally, or even nounally, but I like to plan ahead.

"Grandma" and "Granny" have already been taken by our family's senior matriarchs. Grandy is a fried chicken franchise. And in my opinion, common diminutives such as Nana, Maw-maw, and Mo-mo are too similar to other double-syllabic babyisms such as *caa-caa*, *poo-poo*, and *pee-pee.*

After careful consideration, I've decided Ono is appropriate. It's short, easily pronounceable, and was the first thing I said in response to my daughter's "Guess what! We're going to have a BABY!"

I'm sure I'll adjust to grandmotherhood, feel my heart ripple with joy the first time I see that tiny girl or boy, and be at its beck whenever it calls "Ono."

What Spouse, the prospective twinkle-eyed and belly-tickling grandfather will be known as, has yet to be determined. His choices are similarly limited, but what *he* muttered after Daughter's announcement simply *won't* bear repeating.